Three
Women Poets

Three Women Poets

Renaissance and Baroque

Louise Labé, Gaspara Stampa, and Sor Juana Inés de la Cruz

Poems selected and translated by
Frank J. Warnke

Lewisburg
Bucknell University Press
London and Toronto: Associated University Presses

Associated University Presses
440 Forsgate Drive
Cranbury, NJ 08512

Associated University Presses
25 Sicilian Avenue
London WC1A 2QH, England

Associated University Presses
2133 Royal Windsor Drive
Unit 1
Mississauga, Ontario
Canada L5J 1K5

The paper used in this publication meets the
requirements of the American National
Standard for Permanence of Paper for Printed
Library Materials Z39.48-1984.

Library of Congress Cataloging-in-Publication Data

Three women poets.
  Bibliography: p.
  1. Poetry—Women authors.   2. Poetry—Women authors—
Translations into English.   3. English poetry—Transla-
tions from foreign languages.   I. Labé, Louise, 1526?-
1566.   II. Stampa, Gaspara, ca. 1523-ca. 1554.
III.   Juana Inés de la Cruz, Sister, 1651–1695.
IV. Warnke, Frank J.
PN6109.9.T47   1986   808.81   84-46103
ISBN 0-8387-5089-3 (alk. paper)

Printed in the United States of America

Contents

Acknowledgments

My detailed study of the three poets represented in this volume began in the context of a course on women poets of the Renaissance and Baroque which I taught several times at the University of Washington. Subsequently, at the University of Georgia, I taught these poets in the framework of courses on the Baroque and on the European lyric. (It is ultimately more desirable to absorb these important poets into the general canon of European literature than to treat them in the isolation of a "women poets" course.) I'm grateful to my students for their enthusiastic understanding of the works of these women. More specifically, I'm grateful to the following colleagues or students for much good and helpful conversation: William Clamurro, Betty Jean Craige, Giovanni Guernelli, Franco Lancetti, Anne Paolucci, Richard Poss, Jeanne Prine, Glenda Wall, and Katharina Wilson. Finally, I am indebted to my secretaries Penny Adams and Marigene Banks, not only for their swift and accurate typing but also for their perceptive and sometimes sharp critical comments.

I am grateful to the following for kind permission to reproduce the portraits of the poets:

> Bibliothèque Nationale, Paris (for Louise Labé)
> Rizzoli Editore, Milan (for Gaspara Stampa)
> Fondo de Cultura Económica, Mexico (for Sor Juana Inés
> de la Cruz)

The original texts of the poems by Sor Juana Inés de la Cruz are also reprinted with the kind permission of the Fondo de Cultura Económica.

The following translations from Sor Juana were originally published in Frank J. Warnke, *European Metaphysical Poetry* (New Haven: Yale University Press, 1961): "Green fascination of our human life," "The Rhetoric of Tears," "A Method of Loving." I am grateful to Yale University Press for permission to reprint.

Three
Women Poets

Introduction

To a degree not generally recognized, women shared in the great literary flowering of the two successive ages that we know as the Renaissance and the Baroque. The field in which they contributed the most distinguished work was lyric poetry, and that fact in itself may explain to some extent the failure of even the greatest of these women—Louise Labé, Gaspara Stampa, and Sor Juana Inés de la Cruz—to achieve a broadly international reputation. For, in addition to the literary provincialism that afflicts all national cultures (apart from specialists, how many cultivated speakers of English can name more than a handful of the great writers of Germany and Italy?), the lyric poet suffers from the fact that his or her art is more closely bound to its language than is the art of the dramatist or the novelist. That singularly tight bond is, of course, the despair of any translator of poetry, but despair does not render the challenge any more resistible. Hence the present volume.

The Renaissance (1400–1600 in Italy, 1500–1600 elsewhere in Western Europe) and the Baroque (1600–1700) produced a striking number of distinguished women poets: in Italy Vittoria Colonna, Veronica Gambara, Barbara Torelli, Isabella di Morra, Gaspara Stampa, Veronica Franco, and Tullia d'Aragona; in France Louise Labé, Marguérite de Navarre, Pernette du Guillet and Georgette de Montenay; in the German-speaking world Katharina Regina von Greiffenberg and Sibylle Schwartz; in Holland Maria Tesselschade Visscher; in the Spanish-speaking world the Colombian mystic La Madre Castillo and the great Mexican poet Sor Juana Inés de la Cruz. The English-speaking world of the time does not have as impressive a record. The best women poets of the language—the New England poet Anne Bradstreet, Katherine Philips, and Aphra Behn (better known as a dramatist and writer of fiction)—are, despite felicitous moments, unquestionably minor poets. Such is certainly not the case for Sor Juana, who belongs to world literature, or for

11

Louise Labé and Gaspara Stampa, each of whom has particular merits which cause her to stand out in the literature of her country, even in an age of many great lyric poets.

It is always difficult to be an artist; it is more difficult for a woman to be an artist; and it was especially difficult for a woman to be an artist in the centuries of which we speak. Viewed by the Church as the daughter of Eve, the crooked rib, and the weaker vessel, woman was viewed by the law and civil authorities as a chattel, initially the property of her father, subsequently the property of her husband. The misogynistic polemics of several of the Fathers of the Church do not make very edifying reading, and medieval tales about the comeuppances received by shrewish wives and other uppity females are likely not to seem as sidesplitting to modern people as they presumably were to their original readers. In a society such as that of the Middle Ages and the Renaissance, to be a poet and a woman required both a talent and a determination in excess of anything required of Dr. Johnson's infamous dog on hind legs.

There was, to be sure, an opposed conception of woman, one which manifested itself first in southern France in the late eleventh and early twelfth centuries. I am referring, of course, to the conception associated with the doctrines of courtly love which informed the art of the Provençal troubadours and, subsequently, that of the northern French *trouvères,* the German *Minnesinger,* and the Italian poets of the *dolce stil nuovo.* Much controversy has attended modern investigations of *amour courtois*[1]—with some scholars relating it to the influence of Arabic erotic mysticism, others associating it with the Manichaean tenets of the Albigensian heresy, and still others denying that it ever existed, or ever existed as more than a playful courtly game. Some regard it as a secular displacement of the cult of the Virgin which manifested itself in the European sensibility at about the same time, while others regard that cult itself as a religious displacement of courtly eroticism. Assuming that it did in fact exist—and the evidence, I believe, indicates that it did—it is possible to regard *amour courtois* as being what one might call the revenge of the *anima:* in a cultural situation in which the Establishment systematically denied all worth to the female principle, some force within the male psyche, long repressed and denied, eventually burst forth, affirming not only the value of the female principle but its supreme value, as something to be exalted, obeyed, and worshipped. *Amour courtois* and the cult of Mary are to be regarded, thus, not as causally related phenomena but as parallel phenomena attributable to the same overpowering psychological impulse.

The courtly love attitude could not, of course, contribute in a direct or uncomplicated way to the liberation of the female poet, for that attitude made of woman not the singer but the object of song, not the poet but the muse who inspired the poet. Nevertheless, the Comtesse de Die and other Provençal women wrote troubadour poems, making the necessary adjustments in the standard conventions, and a few generations later an Italian woman known only as the "Compiuta Donzella," the "accomplished damsel," could write poetry instinct with natural lyric grace. Although *amour courtois* could not provide women with an immediately usable poetic language and poetic conventions, it bestowed on them an intrinsic worth which was bound eventually to overcome the restraints against poetic expression.

The Renaissance inherited from the later Middle Ages the courtly attitude toward women and toward sexual love. At the same time, the exaltation of classical antiquity which virtually defines the Renaissance sensibility induced a distrust of medieval authority and precedent together with a somewhat supercilious contempt for medieval attitudes. These newer cultural values may explain how it was that, among the privileged classes, at first in Italy and then elsewhere in western Europe, a new attitude toward the education of women manifested itself. In such circles a female child received essentially the same education as did a male child—a humanistic education, with a stress on Latin (and to some extent Greek), music, rhetoric, and literature. (The education which Sir Thomas More gave his daughters exemplifies this trend, as does—as we shall see—the education received by Louise Labé.) Furthermore, classical learning might find—in the mythological figures of the Muses, in the historical figure of Sappho—further bases for the concept of woman as poet.

But the currency of a more dignified image of woman, the availability of a classical education, and the example of Sappho and the Muses are not enough—either singly or in combination—to make possible the emergence of a female poet of serious artistic stature. For it to be possible, in the Renaissance, I believe the woman had to have, in addition to her innate talents, a certain kind of social identity—any one of four separate kinds, to be more specific: as a *grande dame,* as a *femme savante,* as a *cortigiana onesta,* or as a nun. Although the figure of the *cortigiana onesta* did not exist in Europe before the Renaissance, the other three figures did, and participation in any one of the social identities evoked by those figures made the creation of poetry, for a medieval woman, far more possible than it otherwise would have been. The *grande dame,* of course, in any of the national cultures of Europe, found that the privileges of her station bestowed on her a relatively high degree of freedom to pursue her personal bents—in addition to providing her with the necessary leisure. The inclination might be toward politics, or adultery, or witchcraft, or poetry, but in any event the possibility of personal fulfillment was, for obvious reasons, much higher for the great

13

lady than for her humbler sisters. The freedom which Eleanor of Aquitaine devoted to a number of activities was devoted by Marie de France to poetic composition.

But the medieval bourgeoise too had certain courses of life available which might make literary activity possible. The *femme savante*, the learned lady, was regarded with respect, and that respect in turn led to a toleration of literary activity. The fourteenth-century Christine de Pisan, daughter of an astrologer-physician and herself a physician as well as an exquisitely gifted poet, will serve as a good example of this category. Aristocrat, bourgeoise, and peasant alike had a final course of life which, if it did not specifically encourage poetic composition, at least did not prohibit it. That course of life was the religious. Whatever the rigors of convent life, it allowed time for reflection and meditation, and both the time thus rendered available and the intellectual discipline required by meditation could, and often did, lead to literary production. Sometimes such production was in prose, as in the work of the English mystic Julian of Norwich; equally often it was in metrical form, as in the poems of the thirteenth-century Flemish nun Hadewych.

These three social identities persisted into the Renaissance, though with some erosion of the poetic potential of the learned and religious categories—presumably because, on the one hand, Humanism encouraged the dedication of intellectual energy to specifically artistic or literary ends rather than philosophical or scientific ends, while, on the other hand, the increasingly secular tendencies of society led to a kind of polarization which inhibited the religious person from compromising devotional expression by putting it into verse. (This latter tendency, as we shall see, reverses itself as the Renaissance yields to the Baroque.) The *grande dame* figure continues as a focus of poetic energy, and to it Renaissance culture adds the figure of the *cortigiana onesta*, or "honest courtesan."

Any society which has the bad judgment to split asunder the realms of passionate sexuality, respectable domesticity, and intellectual and cultural companionship is liable to have to invent the category of the honest courtesan—although it is not likely to do so until it has become sophisticated, skeptical in matters of religion, and, most of all, decidedly urban. So it was in fifth-century B.C. Greece. The respectable woman was expected, in a sense required, to be obedient, industrious, available, and dumb—an agent for running the upper-class male's household, bearing his children, and supporting the status quo. In the ideal matron, sexual passion would be as indecorous as brains. (Such, at least, was the theory of the thing; in fact, the presence in Greek literature of such figures as Clytemnaestra and Phaedra suggests the male's panicked recognition that reality was likely to be different.)[2] Men, however, want more than a sluggish domestic tumble for the production of progeny:

14

they are likely to want both passion and the companionship of intellectual peers. For those—and, as we know, there were many—who preferred men, there were homosexual relationships that provided both. For the more relentlessly heterosexual there were whores for sex, but, unfortunately, whores can be as dumb as matrons. Hence the institution of the *hetaira*. The *hetaira* was a prostitute who was capable of providing not only sexual satisfaction but also intellectual companionship. Capable of discoursing at a high cultural level, indeed at a philosophical level, she was thoroughly conversant with music and literature, both as performer and as creator. There is a clear analogy with the traditional Japanese *geisha*, another figure inevitably spawned by a culture which was, like the Greek, both patriarchal and military.

Western Christian society of the Middle Ages was also patriarchal and military, as well as being, as we have seen, officially misogynistic. It is thus not surprising that a *hetaira*-figure eventually makes her appearance and that she appears first in Venice—perhaps the most cosmopolitan, sophisticated, and breezily secular of early Renaissance cities. Whether the emergence of the *cortigiana onesta* has also something to do with Near Eastern influences reaching Venice as a result of commercial relations is a matter for speculation. At any rate, by the 1500s the *cortigiana onesta* was a recognized Venetian institution, enjoying not only toleration but indeed something that amounted to respect. Kings and cardinals were not only among their patrons but also among their admirers and friends. From Venice the institution spread to other northern Italian cities as well as to Lyon, the most Italianate of the French capitals. It did not spread to Germanic northern Europe—probably because, the Renaissance having reached those cultures not much before the Reformation, the more intransigent and rigorous morality of Protestantism discouraged its development as the permissive Catholicism of the Renaissance had not. (The *cortigiana onesta* did not, we may note, survive the advent of Counter-Reformation Catholicism.)

In what did the *onestà* of the *cortigiana onesta* consist? Primarily in the fact that she had one lover at a time, her protector and patron, to whom she was, at least in theory, true as long as the relationship lasted. In a less tangible sense she was honest because, unlike a whore, she did not pursue the simple commerce of offering sex for money. In a far more complex way she offered, along with sex, intellectual and cultural companionship in return for a support which included not only money but also a position of quasi respectability. It is the loss of such a position, perhaps, to which Gaspara Stampa alludes in one of her complaints to the untrue Collaltino di Collalto, who has abandoned her:

> Credete ch'io sia Ercol o Sansone
> a poter sostener tanto dolore,

15

giovane e donna e fuor d'ogni ragione,
massime essendo qui senza 'l mio core
e senza voi a mia difensione,
onde mi suol venir forza e vigore?

Am I Hercules or Samson, do you suppose,
To bear such sorrow now that we're apart?
I'm young, a woman, half out of my mind,
And, most of all, I'm here without my heart,
You being gone, in whom I used to find
Defense, who were for me strength and repose.

Gaspara Stampa, the greatest woman poet of Renaissance Italy, was almost certainly a *cortigiana onesta*. Her fellow Venetians Tullia d'Aragona and Veronica Franco were assuredly such. The artistic accomplishment of these women at least equals and probably excels that of the Italian *grandes dames* of the period—Vittoria Colonna, Veronica Gambara, Barbara Torelli, and the unfortunate Isabella di Morra. The stature of their accomplishment suggests the degree to which the courtesan status encouraged poetic creation, and the suggestion is reinforced by a consideration of the French women poets of the Renaissance: of the three most important, one—Marguérite de Navarre—was the grandest of *grandes dames*; the other two—Pernette du Guillet and Louise Labé—were both bourgeoises, both Lyonnaises, and, in the opinion of most modern authorities, both honest courtesans on the Venetian model.

We have seen that the institution of the *cortigiana onesta* did not spread to northern Europe. Nor did it spread to the Iberian peninsula, possibly, once again, because of stricter codes of sexual morality. Spain and Portugal were and remained, of course, rigidly Catholic, but, even before the Counter-Reformation, Catholicism there had little of the casualness of High Renaissance Italy—perhaps because the centuries of conflict with the Moors had imposed a kind of siege mentality hospitable to fanaticism. Neither great ladies nor courtesans appear among the literary women of the Spanish- and Portuguese-speaking world; the sole category represented appears to be that of the nun.

The greatest literary figure among Spanish women of the sixteenth century—Santa Teresa de Ávila—does not rank among the great poets. Her occasional metrical compositions have charm and sweetness, but they clearly did not receive her major attention—that being, presumably, reserved for the works that give her her position among the major figures both in mysticism and in the history of Spanish prose. The most distinguished woman poet of the Iberian peninsula during the centuries of the Renaissance and the Baroque is probably the Portuguese nun Soror Violante do Ceu.

Spanish-speaking America produced during the Baroque at least two women poets of importance. One, the Colombian mystic known as La Madre Castillo, wrote accounts of her spiritual experiences in both prose and verse; in both media her expression is hectic and extravagant but memorable and often impressive. The other, the Mexican woman born Juana de Asbaje but better known under her religious name as Sor Juana Inés de la Cruz, is one of the major poets of world literature and the last great figure of the Spanish Baroque. In the present volume her lyric work will be more generously represented than even that of those superb poets Louise Labé and Gaspara Stampa.

The three poets represented differ in a number of ways. Louise Labé and Gaspara Stampa are exclusively poets of human love (Gaspara, it is true, wrote religious lyrics as well as love lyrics, but the former are consistently conceived either as passionate expressions of her repentance for her enslavement to earthly passion or as pretty clear religious displacements of a passion which continues to reveal its sexual bases). Louise Labé is above all the poet of physical desire, but her extraordinary intensity of tone more than compensates for her narrow range of theme. In Louise's[3] lyrics, effectively, only her passion and the beloved exist; there is little indication that anything else exists in her life—neither the mundane world, nor politics, nor the claims of the Christian religion. Her *Elégie III* does, it is true, boast of her learning, her skill with the needle, and her martial prowess, but only to speak of how meaningless these things have become to her after the terrible approach of the god of love. Gaspara Stampa, in contrast, expresses her overwhelming sexual passion in a context of awareness of competing values—primarily those of the Christian religion. In her *canzoniere* she stresses, for example, the coincidence of episodes in her love with the feasts of the Christian year (she first met Collalto, according to her account, on Christmas Day—as Petrarch first saw Laura on Good Friday). Or she practices, in her love poems, a conscious and extreme blasphemy, elevating her lover above God and, at times, specifically comparing her vision of that mortal with the beatific vision enjoyed by the angels above.

Despite the differences between the lyric work of Louise and Gaspara, there are interesting similarities, in addition to the supercharged eroticism that characterizes both. There is, for example, the conception of a female deity to whom each poet addresses her complaints—Louise to Venus, or the Evening Star, in "Clere Venus, qui erres par les Cieus"; Gaspara, in "Io son de l'aspettar omai si stanca," to a curious figure who combines the identities of the moon (and hence Artemis) and of Death, figured here not as the familiar Grim Reaper of northern tradition but rather as a pale woman. The female deity, without any specific competition in Louise Labé's work, is, in Gaspara Stampa's, in competition with Christ—but Gaspara seems to have more hope of comfort in the female

17

. The female deity does not, as far as I know, appear in Sor Juana's
but the Mexican nun composed the most specifically feminist
to be found in the *oeuvres* of all three poets—the famous *redondillas*
e stupidity of men, who devote their energy to seducing women
hen reproach them for not being chaste.

There is little or no Petrarchism in Louise Labé, and she thus avoids
one of the major technical problems for women love poets of the Renais-
sance—the application to their amorous situation of a set of conventions
specifically developed to articulate the predicament of a male lover of a
cold, distant, and virtuous woman. Gaspara Stampa, as an Italian lyric
poet of the Cinquecento, is inevitably Petrarchan, and the enterprise
with which she adapts and modifies the male conventions to her own
situation is one of the most impressive aspects of her artistic achieve-
ment. She retains from Petrarch the pose of adoration for a cold and
distant love, but she makes it clear that his coldness and distance are
aspects not of his chastity or moral superiority but rather of the fact that,
having enjoyed his mistress, he has abandoned her. Physical desire,
which Gaspara expresses almost as vitally as does Louise, is located not
in fantasy or daydream, as in Petrarch, but in the memory of the joy of
past fulfillment. Unlike Louise, whose lyric *oeuvre* consists of a scant
three elegies and 24 sonnets, Gaspara wrote a full *canzoniere* consisting of
"rime d'amore" (221 sonnets, 19 madrigals, and five "capitoli") and "rime
varie" (62 sonnets and five canzoni). The conspicuously larger output
inevitably means that Gaspara is able to investigate the various dimen-
sions of love more thoroughly than is Louise.

Robert Graves has suggested that all true poetry is inspired by the
Muse, that is to say, in Graves's terms, by the female principle most
definitively embodied in the Great Goddess worshiped by a wide variety
of religious cults.[4] The courtly or Petrarchan male poet, in his posture of
devotion to the elevated, distant, and virtuous lady, his Beatrice or
Laura, is simultaneously expressing erotic longing, transmuting that
longing into religious transcendence, and establishing contact with the
magical roots of his own creativity. But, as Graves asks in his essay on
Sor Juana, where is the female poet to find her Muse?[5] The concept of a
male Muse is clearly ridiculous, and it is worth noting that, in Gaspara
Stampa's *canzoniere*, the unfaithful Collalto in no sense fulfills a Muse-
function. He is the agency, the occasion, through which Gaspara's cre-
ative and erotic energy is liberated, but that energy has its ultimate
source in Gaspara herself. She is, as Graves remarks of Sor Juana (and
Sappho) herself the Muse, and the double burden of inspiring and being
inspired demands a singular kind of heroism.[6]

Among the most important modifications of Petrarchism effected by
the Venetian poet is the displacement of moral superiority from the

distant love to the complaining lover, a displacement which is paradoxical in that it coexists with Gaspara's consistent posture of self-abasement and her equally consistent praise of Collalto's superior qualities. As Justin Vitiello remarks,[7] the little courtesan, abandoned, sinful, full of despair, is ultimately in a position to affirm her own moral worth. She knows, as did Socrates, that the lover is nobler than the beloved. Perhaps only the poet who is also the Muse can achieve such knowledge.

Sor Juana Inés de la Cruz—billed in her early publications as "la décima Musa" ("the tenth Muse")—differs from Louise Labé and Gaspara Stampa in a number of respects. To begin with, her poetic themes are not limited to sexual love, nor is her poetic output restricted to the lyric. In addition to a vast number of lyrics on a wide range of subjects—amorous, philosophical, religious, and satiric—she wrote dramatic works embracing genres as diverse as the comedy and the *auto sacramental*. Her *Respuesta a Sor Filotea de la Cruz* is a monument of Spanish prose as well as an exemplary piece of argumentation and an eloquent plea for the freedom to learn. A further source of variety in Sor Juana's work is the fact that, like most Spanish poets of the *siglo de oro*, she composed lyrics in two distinct and altogether separate categories of metrical form: the first category is made up of poems written in measures such as the sonnet, which, originally Italian, had become general European forms; the second category consists of poems written in the indigenous Spanish forms—*romances, redondillas, villancicos*, etc.—which were to remain always confined to Spanish (and Portuguese) poetry. Like Lope de Vega and Góngora before her, Sor Juana proved a master (if that is the right word) in both categories.

There is another significant difference between Sor Juana and the two other poets of this volume. Whereas Louise Labé and Gaspara Stampa seem in their love lyrics to be speaking quite directly from their own experience, Sor Juana eludes us. Perhaps her own amorous experience is reflected in her love lyrics, as her own religious emotions and philosophical speculations may be reflected in other lyrics. But we cannot know for certain. Every inch the artist, she escapes us always, refusing to abide our question. The world she presents us with may be entirely a world of fiction. If so, I can picture the Mexican nun replying, with a mocking smile, "So what?" or the Spanish equivalent thereof.

Fictionality, fantasy, and a kind of pervasive playfulness characterize Sor Juana's lyric work, and those features are traceable not only to her individual temperament but also to the cultural period of which she is a distinctive product. Louise Labé and Gaspara Stampa are Renaissance artists, fully typical of their age; Sor Juana is a Baroque artist, and no less typical as such. The definition of Baroque has long been a vexed question of cultural history,[8] and much ink has been squandered in drawing distinctions between that period and the Renaissance that preceded it (or, for some authorities, between the Baroque and the period of Mannerism that they see as falling between Renaissance and Baroque).[9] I have argued elsewhere that such Baroque features as extravagance, intellectuality, wittiness, and a love of paradox and contradiction are rooted in a deeply felt conviction of the illusory nature of all earthly phenomena, a conviction that derives partly from the erosion of the older symbolic world view of the Middle Ages and the Renaissance, partly from the intensified religious sensibility fostered by the Reformation and the Counter-Reformation.[10] (The purely infraliterary phenomenon of reaction against a previously dominant style ought not to be ignored as a factor contributing to the formation of the Baroque style.)[11] Whatever the sources of Baroque art, that art is distinguished by an assumption that what the free imagination creates has the status of truth, however odd that creation may seem. Sor Juana's poetry, with its elaborate conceits, its paradoxes, its extravagant imagery, and its delicate but unshakable equilibrium between levity and profound seriousness, is, like that of Andrew Marvell, a major achievement of the Baroque imagination.

Taken at face value, Gaspara Stampa's *canzoniere* is a straightforward account of the ecstasies and sufferings caused her by her love for Count Collalto. In a more devious way, it is possible that Collalto is the *occasion* for Gaspara's poetry, her feelings for him deliberately and cunningly heightened and manipulated in order to create an emotional state that will make the writing of poetry possible. The same alternatives are present in the case of Louise Labé and the unnamed object of her sexual passion. But for both poets there is, one assumes, a core, a nub, of biographical actuality about which the poetic work crystallizes. In the case of Sor Juana we cannot be certain of even that. The supposition that she had one or more ardent love affairs before entering the convent at the age of seventeen can be neither refuted nor sustained, nor can the assumption of some commentators that there was a Lesbian relationship between Juana and the vicereine of Mexico, whose favorite she was. Perhaps the profound and delicate understanding of sexual passion that permeates her love lyrics is the product of her experience; perhaps it is the product simply of her extraordinary intelligence. It remains possible that the only significant romance in Sor Juana's life was her unending love affair with language and thought, a devotion stronger perhaps than her devotion to God.

It is her love of language and the games the intellect can play with it that makes Sor Juana one of the definitive poets of the Baroque. Technical virtuosity and the constant play of wit characterize all her poetry, and these features reach an extreme in her most ambitious poem, the

Sueño (Dream), a cosmic meditation on epistemology. Deliberately modeled on the work of Luís de Góngora, one of the most opaque as well as one of the greatest of Spanish poets, the *Sueño* shows Sor Juana to be her master's equal in the creation of intricate, allusive, and ambiguous verse, and perhaps his superior in philosophical depth.

The *Sueño* poses particular, perhaps insuperable problems for the metrical translator. It is a long poem—975 lines—and I have rendered only about the first fourth of it, in order to give the English-speaking reader at least an impression of it. In my translation I have tried to maintain the metrical pattern of the original but have cast it into lines of unrhymed English verse. (The original is a *silva*, a poem in strophes of unequal length rhymed irregularly, with some lines left unrhymed— rather in the manner of Milton's "Lycidas.") My treatment of this poem thus differs from that given to the other poems in this volume, which I have translated into rhymed English verse. A great many of the poems are sonnets. These I have translated into English sonnets—generally preserving the envelope-rhymed octaves of the originals, but occasionally using an *abab cdcd* rhyme scheme instead. I have not attempted to render the sestet rhyme schemes precisely, but have in most cases employed a Petrarchan sestet of one form or another. Occasionally, as in Gaspara Stampa's "Io non v'invidio punto, angeli santi," I have abandoned the Petrarchan sestet in favor of a sestet concluding with a couplet—simply because I thought it sounded good and caught the feeling of the original.

In essaying verse translations of these poems, I have not flattered myself with the illusion that they recapture, or even come very close to recapturing, the qualities of the originals. In that case, one might ask, why not simply provide a straightforward prose translation, in which semantic accuracy is the only objective? My reason for rejecting that approach—an approach that could be eloquently defended—is that Louise, Gaspara, and Sor Juana did, after all, write poems, a fact that prose translation obscures. The obscuring of that fact outweighs, in my view, the perhaps more precise rendition of meaning that prose might make possible. True precision in translation, whatever the mode employed, is an unattainable goal, even if it must be the goal toward which the translator always strives.

The *raison d'être* of this book is to make three great poets of the past more accessible to modern English-speaking people. The reader who has French, Italian, Spanish, or all three languages won't need my translations; some readers will, and I hope they will like them. In any case, here are the poems, and they are sufficient evidence, I submit, to warrant a revision of the canon of world poetry—a revision which ought to elevate Sor Juana to her proper place as one of the world's greatest

21

lyric poets and ought to establish Gaspara Stampa and Louise Labé as two of the finest lyric poets of the Renaissance.

NOTES

1. See Denis de Rougemont, *Love in the Western World*, rev. ed. (Garden City, N.Y., 1957).

2. Virginia Woolf reminds us of this fact on several occasions. See, for example, *A Room of One's Own* (New York, 1929), pp. 71–99.

3. In these pages, as in the biographical headnotes, I sometimes refer to these poets as "Louise," "Gaspara," and "Sor Juana." This should in no sense be taken as paralleling the condescending practice of some now outdated biographers and critics who call Emily Brontë "Emily" or Virginia Woolf "Virginia." My practice, rather, abides by Italian Renaissance usage or by ecclesiastical custom with regard to members of religious orders. In other words, I use the first names with the same formality and respect with which we use the first names of Leonardo da Vinci, Michelangelo Buonarroti, Dante Alighieri, or San Juan de la Cruz.

4. Robert Graves, *The White Goddess*, enl. ed. (New York, 1972).

5. Robert Graves, "Juana de Asbaje," in *The Crowning Privilege* (London, 1955), p. 166.

6. Ibid.

7. In "Gaspara Stampa: The Ambiguities of Martyrdom," *Modern Language Notes* 90 (1975): 58–71.

8. Among the most important treatments are: René Wellek, *Concepts of Criticism* (New Haven, 1963), pp. 69–127; Helmut Hatzfeld, *Estudios sobre el barroco* (Madrid, 1964); Odette de Mourgues, *Metaphysical, Baroque, and Précieux Poetry* (Oxford, 1953); Peter Skrine, *The Baroque* (New York, 1978). My own view is expressed in F. J. Warnke, *Versions of Baroque* (New Haven, 1972).

9. See, for example, Hatzfeld, *Estudios;* Wylie Sypher, *Four Stages of Renaissance Style* (Garden City, N.Y., 1955); and Arnold Hauser, *Mannerism: The Crisis of the Renaissance and the Origin of Modern Art*, 2 vols. (London, 1965).

10. Warnke, *Versions of Baroque*, pp. 21–65.

11. F. J. Warnke, "Baroque Once More: Notes on a Literary Period," *New Literary History* 1, no. 2 (1970): 145–62.

Louise Labé
(1522?–1566)

The date of Louise Labé's birth is not known with certainty. Boy[1] places it between extreme termini of 1515 and 1524; most modern authorities agree on 1522 or 1523 as a probable date. Her father was a prosperous rope-maker named Pierre Charly, also called Labé; her mother was, in all probability, the second of Pierre's three wives, the widow Etiennette Deschamps, whom he had married in around 1515 and who died in 1524. It is likely that the poet was born not in Lyon, the city with which she is so closely associated, but in the nearby village of Parcieu-en-Dombes, where Pierre had a property. She received an excellent education and was, as an adolescent, already accomplished in languages (particularly Italian and Latin), music, and verse composition, as well as in the more conventionally accepted female activities of needlework and embroidery. Horsemanship and the practice of arms were also among her attainments, as a later passage of this sketch will make clear.

The liberality and depth of her education may seem surprising to modern readers, in view of Louise's bourgeois origins and of what we may assume to have been sixteenth-century attitudes toward the proper role of woman. What should be remembered, in addition to her apparently having been Pierre's favorite among his many offspring, is the atmosphere of the city of Lyon at the dawn of the Renaissance, when new ideas, new forms of art, and a new and remarkably zestful sense of the possibilities of human existence were everywhere apparent. The source of these novelties was, of course, Italy, where, since the time of Petrarch and Boccaccio in the fourteenth century, the new world view had been progressively ousting the values and assumptions of medieval culture. Situated on the confluence of the Rhone and the Saone, at the

23

Louise Labé

great crossroads of the trade routes between North and South and East and West, Lyon was in a position to receive Italian influences more immediately and intensely than any other of the important French cities (and sixteenth-century Lyon was, in population and affluence, a close rival to Paris). Dissemination of the new learning was furthered by the importance of Lyon as a printing and publishing center. Furthermore, Lyon had been, during the fifteenth century, the staging area for the successive French military invasions of northern Italy. In addition to merchandise, in addition to booty, Italian businessmen and returning French captains brought with them ideas, assumptions, and a whole cultural idiom—the Humanist orientation toward classical antiquity, the amorous attitudes that Petrarch had refined and codified from those of the *dolce stil nuovo*, the poetic forms which that poet had perfected in order to express those attitudes, the teachings of the Platonic Academy of Florence, and, in short, a feeling of freedom and openness to innovation which perhaps explains both Louise's humanistic education and the assured articulateness that characterizes all her poetic work. Indeed, in Renaissance Italy, in circles of the nobility and the upper bourgeoisie, the idea that girls should receive the same kind of education as boys had gained wide acceptance. Presumably this belief too had been imported to Lyon. By 1522, the probable year of Louise's birth, Lyon had become a Renaissance city while Paris was still largely medieval.

Louise Labé's ultimate poetic master is obviously Petrarch—though she is not "Petrarchan" in a conventional sense—but her more immediate master was the greatest of the Renaissance poets of Lyon, Maurice Scève. His influence appears to have been more pedagogical and inspirational than technical, however, for there is little resemblance between the straightforward, passionate verse of Louise Labé and the subtle, intellectual, extraordinarily complex art of Scève, that great exponent of a kind of proto-Mannerism. And, though the relationship with Scève must surely have strengthened Louise's Petrarchism, the younger poet's work is entirely free of the Platonism that is such an important part of Scève poetic stance.

To call Louise's poetry "straightforward" is in no sense to imply that it is simple or naïve. Like all good Renaissance poets, Louse is an accomplished rhetorician and a self-conscious artist. In the elegies and the sonnets alike she is clearly aware of the implications of genre and the conventions that lie behind it. Indeed, the effect of straightforwardness, of emotional directness, that has captivated four centuries of readers is to be attributed to her artistry rather than to the strength of her passions *tout court*. The road to bad poetry is paved with good emotions; good poetry requires that those emotions—whether real or fictive—be transmuted by art, and that Louise could do superbly.

If there is little resemblance between Louise's poems and those of Scève, there is scarcely more to be found between her work and that of the other eminent French poets of the mid sixteenth century, almost all of whom she knew personally. Some of them—Olivier de Magny, Pontus de Tyard, and Pernette du Guillet (herself the beloved of Scève and the inspiration, according to tradition, of his *Délie*)—were personal friends. Others—Marot,Ronsard, Du Bellay, Baïf—were acquaintances. But her work shows neither the lingering medievalism of Pernette, nor Du Bellay's Platonism, nor Ronsard's virtuosity and versatility. Her exclusive concentration on the theme of physical passion and her distinctive tone of desperate intensity give her a unique position among French Renaissance poets.

Some time around 1543 Louise Labé married Ennemond Perrin, some thirty years her senior and, like her father, a rope-maker. Hence the sobriquet so frequently applied to her in her own time—"La Belle Cordière," "the beautiful rope-maker." It is unlikely that the good bourgeois Perrin was the inspiration for Louise's art: among other things, most of her poems were written well after her marriage, and they can scarcely be construed as implying a domestic or marital situation. The identity of the recipient of Louise's ardent sighs—if, indeed, he actually existed at all—remains a mystery, although legend has been generous in supplying nominees for that honor—Olivier de Magny, Pontus de Tyard, and, of all people, King Henri II, the very same monarch whose service in arms had lured Collaltino di Collalto away from the embraces of his devoted and persistent Gaspara Stampa. The royal liaison may safely be dismissed as legendary; there is no evidence to support its existence. Magny assuredly had an attachment to the poet; there exists an unpleasant poetic satire of his against Ennemond Perrin which both suggests that the latter had resented Magny's attentions to his wife and casts considerable doubt on Louise's virtue. Tyard contributed gallant dedicatory verse to the first edition of Labé's poems, but given the nature of Renaissance complimentary verse, we are not justified in assuming an emotional relationship of any particular intimacy. It is, of course, also possible that Labé's poems derive retrospectively from the adolescent love referred to in her *Elégie III*—or, as has already been suggested, that they have reference to a fictitious or fantasy figure.

Why does one, in any case, devote time to idle speculation as to the love life of Louise Labé? Perhaps because most previous writers on that poet have done so. Perhaps because of an innate fascination, on the part of a male writer, with the amorous life of a female artist—even one dead more than four hundred years. Perhaps—more defensibly—a curiosity inevitable in the case of an artist whose sole subject was physical love. Be that as it may, most scholarship and criticism devoted to the Lyonnaise poet has occupied itself strenuously with the question of her love life and, by extension, with the question of her sexual morals. Some contemporaneous authorities refer to her (as well as to Pernette du Guillet) as a courtesan; others extoll her virtue in hyperbolic terms. Although it is impossible to be certain of the truth of the matter, it seems to me to lie somewhere between the two extremes: Louise Labé was assuredly not a whore, but she was not the ideal of conventional feminine virtue glorified by some of her nineteenth-century editors. Given some of the sixteenth-century evidence—Magny's satire, the scurrilous anonymous *Chanson nouvelle de la Belle Cordière*, the tone of faintly leering respect that informs so many of the complimentary verses in the *Oeuvres*—I suspect that she was, like her Italian coeval Gaspara Stampa, a *cortigiana onesta*, or "honest courtesan."[2] The social and cultural position of such a figure was, as I have maintained in my Introduction, anomalous and ambiguous. Lyon, with its strongly Italianate culture, was no doubt more prepared to recognize the institution than was Paris or any other more northerly city, though less prepared than was Venice, a city which, with its cosmopolitan and half-oriental sophistication, was uniquely capable of accepting and respecting a kind of woman whose way of life was in flat defiance of all the pieties of church and state.

John Calvin was in no doubt as to Louise's sexual morals: she was a common whore, *plebeia meretrix*.[3] But, then, what else was the sour theocrat of Geneva to make of a beautiful woman, a Catholic, who presided over a salon frequented by learned and creative men, who wrote passionate love poetry that shows no trace of a sense of guilt, and who, worst of all, was in the habit of wearing male attire? This last offense, for Calvin, said it all, for it was an abominable thing, contrary to Scripture, and any woman who so offended must surely be a whore.

Mention is frequently made of Louise's male dress and of her skill at horsemanship and the use of weapons. She herself, in *Elégie III,* writes as follows:

> He who had seen me proudly ride to war,
> Couch my lance, take on the furious jar
> Of combat armed, strike, urge my glorious mount,
> Might well have taken me for Bradamant,
> Ruggiero's love, or for Marfisa bold,
> Such martial virtue did I then uphold.

This passage, together with several contemporaneous references, has given rise to a charming legend, which must probably be dismissed as no more than that—that the poet, under the name "le Capitaine Loys," took part in François I's campaign against the Spanish near Perpignan and distinguished herself in combat. Far more likely is the explanation given by Boy[4] and others—that Louise Labé took part in a tournament held in or near Lyon either in 1542, when the dauphin, later Henri II, passed through on his way to lead the king's troops against the Spanish, or in 1548, when Henri, by that time himself king, made a festive appearance in Lyon. In any case, Louise appears to have been no mean swordswoman, and this touch of tomboyism seems to have intensified rather than diminished the charm she exerted upon her contemporaries.

In 1555 the works of Louise Labé were published in Lyon: three elegies, twenty-four sonnets,and a prose dialogue entitled *Le débat de Folie et d'Amour.* Three further editions, based on the first, appeared the next year. After that we know little about her fortunes. The anonymous *Chanson nouvelle de la Belle Cordière* was circulating in 1557; Magny's abusive poem was written in 1559; Ennemond Perin died some time in the early 1560s. In April 1565, "sick in bed" at the lodgings in Lyon of the Florentine Thomas Fortini, Louise Labé executed her last will and testament. A year later she died, possibly of the plague, at her country residence in Parcieu.

The poetry of Louise Labé has never lacked admirers, including scholarly ones. As I have previously remarked, much of the attention given her concentrates on her morals and her way of life, often to the exclusion of her art;[5] this is regrettable, in view of the quality of that art. For Louise Labé is not merely a good poet; she is one of the finest of French Renaissance lyrists (in the sixteenth century only Scève, Ronsard, and Du Bellay are incontestably her superiors, and she is much more distinguished than Pernette du Guillet, with whose name hers is often linked). Her poetic output is, of course, small, but the level of achievement is consistently high. The elegies handle the decasyllabic couplet with flexibility, ease, and vehement expressive force. The sonnets show a complete mastery of the form (and it should be noted that Louise had very few predecessors in the writing of French sonnets), and they investigate with thoroughness and with remarkable emotional concentration the theme of physical passion to which they are exclusively devoted. In contrast to Gaspara Stampa, who frequently expresses her amorous longings and complaints in a framework of Christian belief, Louise articulates a poetic vision devoid of religious and philosophical dimensions alike: the only things in it that are real are the unsatisfied soul and the achingly longing body that houses it.

These impressionistic observations recapitulate what has so often been praised in Louise's poetry—directness, passion, and sincerity. Though I would not deny the presence of these qualities, it seems to me important to note that they are communicated through superb craftmanship and accomplished rhetoric. In her dedication of her *Works* to her young woman friend Clémence de Bourges, Louise herself indicates two motives for publication—the desire to encourage other women to "elevate their spirits above their distaffs and spindles" and to demonstrate to the men who have oppressed them that women are capable of great achievement in the arts and sciences, and the conviction that the capturing of emotional experience in verse bestows on it a permanence otherwise impossible.[6] Passionate Louise Labé no doubt was; simple she was certainly not. Passion and intellect combined to make her a great lyric poet.

NOTES

1. Louise Labé, *Oeuvres*, ed. Charles Boy (Geneva: Slatkine Reprints, 1968—reprint of the edition of Paris, 1887, 2 vols.), 2:30.

2. This view is strongly supported by Dorothy O'Connor, *Louise Labé: Sa vie et son oeuvre* (Geneva: Slatkine Reprints, 1972—reprint of the edition of Paris, 1926), pp. 82–91.

3. See Boy, 2:100–101.

4. Boy, 2:38–42.

5. Among the exceptions to this tendency are O'Connor, *Louise Labé,* and Lawrence E. Harvey, *The Aesthetics of the Renaissance Love Sonnet: An Essay on the Art of the Sonnet in the Poetry of Louise Labé* (Geneva: Droz, 1962).

6. Boy, 1:3–6.

O longs desirs, O esperances vaines,
　　Tristes soupirs et larmes coutumieres
　　A engendrer de moy maintes rivieres,
　　Don mes deus yeus sont sources et fontaines:

O cruautez, ô durtez inhumaines,
　　Piteus regars des celestes lumieres:
　　Du coeur transi ô passions premieres,
　　Estimez vous croitre encore mes peines?

Qu'encor Amour sur moy son arc essaie,
　　Que nouveaus feus me gette et nouveaus dars:
　　Qu'il se despite, et pis qu'il pourra face:
Car ie suis tant navree en toutes pars,
　　Que plus en moy une nouvelle plaie,
　　Pour m'empirer ne pourroit trouver place.

———————————

Clere Venus, qui erres par les Cieus,
　　Entens ma voix qui en pleins chantera,
　　Tant que ta face au haut du Ciel luira,
　　Son long travail et souci ennuieus.

Mon oeil veillant s'atendrira bien mieus,
　　Et plus de pleurs te voyant gettera.
　　Mieus mon lit mol de larmes baignera,
　　De ses travaus voyant témoins tes yeus.

Donq des humains sont les lassez esprits
　　De dous repos et de sommeil espris.
　　J'endure mal tant que le Soleil luit:
Et quand ie suis quasi toute cassee,
　　Et que me suis mise en mon lit lassee,
　　Crier me faut mon mal toute la nuit.

———————————

On voit mourir toute chose animee
Lors que du corps l'ame sutile part:

O long desires, O hopes so keen and vain,
O melancholy sighs, familiar tears;
My face the aspect of a river bears,
My eyes the fountains whence it springs again.

O harshness, O inhuman cruelties,
O piteous glances which the stars impart:
O primal passions of my shattered heart,
Do you think more sorrows can my being seize?

Let Cupid try again on me his bow,
Let him new arrows and more flames compound,
Let him grow wrathful, let him vent his anger:
In every part so many scars I show
That he can't make my anguish any stronger:
A place for one more wound cannot be found.

———————————

Bright Venus, you who wander through the sky,
Hear my voice which, while you shine above,
Will sing the plaints provoked in me by love,
The torment long, the pain of which I sigh.

My wakeful eye will better feel its grief
From seeing you, and more tears will be shed,
Tears that will bathe in sorrow my soft bed,
Knowing that you will witness no relief.

Now all weary human spirits rest,
Seized by sweet sleep and natural repose;
But I, who suffer while the sun is shining,
Lie down at night and, by my cares oppressed
And broken, know no respite from my woes,
The whole night long my agony repining.

———————————

We see that every living thing must die,
When the subtle soul from the body doth depart:

31

Je suis le corps, toy la meilleure part:
Ou es tu donq, ô âme bien aymée?

Ne me laissez pas si long temps pamee
Pour me sauver après viendrois trop tard.
Las, ne mets point ton corps en ce hazart:
Rens lui sa part et moitié estimee.

Mais fais, Ami, que ne soit dangereuse
Cette rencontre et revuë amoureuse,
L'accompagnant, non de severité,
Non de rigueur: mais de grace amiable,
Qui doucement me rende ta beauté,
Jadis cruelle, à présent favorable.

———————————

Tout aussi tot que ie commence à prendre
    Dens le mol lit le repos desiré,
    Mon triste esprit hors de moy retiré
    S'en va vers toy incontinent se rendre.

Lors m'est avis que dedens mon sein tendre
    Ie tiens le bien, ou i'ay tant aspiré,
    Et pour lequel i'ay si haut souspiré,
    Que de sanglots ay souvent cuidé fendre.

O dous sommeil, ô nuit à moy heureuse!
    Plaisant repos, plein de tranquilité,
    Continuez toutes les nuiz mon songe:
Et si iamais ma povre ame amoureuse
    Ne doit avoir de bien en verité,
    Faites au moins qu'elle en ait en mensonge.

———————————

Quand i'apperçoy ton blond chef couronné
D'un laurier verd, faire un Lut si bien pleindre,

I am the body, you my better part:
Where are you, soul, for which I longing sigh?

Don't leave me here so long in swooning pain;
You'll come too late to save me, if you wait.
Don't leave your body in such perilous state,
But let it have its well-loved half again.

But please, dear friend, don't let that amorous meeting
Be marred by coldness and by cruel despite;
Instead of rigor show your lovely grace;
One thing alone I cannot help entreating:
When I see again that much-belovèd face,
Be it not severe, but tender to my plight.

————————

From the very moment that I start to find
My wished-for rest, lying in the soft bed,
My mournful spirit straight to you is led
To give itself, my body left behind.

Then it is clear that in my tender breast
I have the joy for which I've so much cried,
For which so long and desperately I've sighed
That I've thought the sobs would cause my heart to burst.

O slumber sweet, O night so kind to me!
Delightful rest, full of tranquil peace
Return and give me every night my dreaming;
And if my poor impassioned soul must be
Denied forever any true release,
Grant at least that it may keep the seeming.

————————

When I behold you, your blond tresses crowned
With laurel green, and hear you play the lute

Que tu pourrois à te suiure contreindre
Arbres et rocs: quand ie te vois orné,

Et de vertus dix mile environné,
Au chef d'honneur plus haut que nul ateindre:
Et des plus hauts les louenges esteindre:
Lors dit mon cœur en soy passionné:

Tant de vertus qui te font estre aymé,
Qui de chacun te font estre estimé,
Ne te pourroient aussi bien faire aymer?
Et aioutant à ta vertu louable
Ce nom encor de m'estre pitoyable,
De mon amour doucement t'enflamer?

———————————

Lut, compagnon de ma calamité,
    De mes soupirs témoin irreprochable,
    De mes ennuis controlleur veritable,
    Tu as souuent auec moy lamanté:

Et tant le pleur piteus t'a molesté,
    Que commençant quelque son delectable,
    Tu le rendois tou soudein lamentable,
    Feignant le ton que plein avoit chanté.

Et si te veus efforcer au contraire,
    Tu te destens et si me contreins taire:
    Mais me voyant tendrement soupirer,
Donnant faveur à ma tant triste pleinte:
    En mes ennuis me plaire suis contreinte,
    Et d'un dous mal douce fin esperer.

———————————

Oh si i'estois en ce beau sein ravie
    De celui là pour lequel vois mourant:

34

Till rocks and trees are plucked up by the root
To follow its complaints, see you renowned

Of all, while many thousand virtues ring you,
And I see you, ahead of all, attain the peak,
And hear how all your praises loudest speak—
Then must my heart, by passion driven, sing you:

These countless virtues, making you so loved
By everyone, these things that make you praised—
Could they not make you just as well a lover?
Thus higher yet your honor would be raised,
Were you by pity so to love me moved,
And for my sweet love an answering flame discover.

———————

Lute, companion of my wretched state,
True witness of my never-ceasing sighs,
Faithful scribe of all my grieving cries,
In lamentation you have been my mate;

My piteous sighs have caused you such distress
That often you've been forced to change your strains,
Replacing your delectable refrains
With notes that my tormented mood express.

And if I would compel your former measure,
Your strings growing slack, you force me to be still;
But when you see me tenderly complain,
You give approval to my grieving pleasure,
And I'm obliged to yield unto your will,
Still hoping for sweet outcome from sweet pain.

———————

Oh, that I could be crushed to that dear breast
Of him for whom in every way I die!

Si avec lui vivre le demeurant
De mes cours jours ne m'empeschoit enuie:

Si m'acollant me disoit, chere Amie,
Contentons nous l'un l'autre, s'asseurant
Que ia tempeste, Euripe, ne Courant
Ne nous pourra desiondre en notre vie:

Si de mes bras le tenant acollé,
Comme du Lierre est l'arbre encercelé,
La mort venoit, de mon aise envieuse:
Lors que souef plus il me baiseroit,
Et mon esprit sur ses levres fuiroit,
Bien ie mourrois, plus que vivante, hereuse.

Tant que mes yeus pourront larmes espandre,
A l'heur passé avec toy regretter:
Et qu'aus sanglots et soupirs resister
Pourra ma voix, et un peu faire entendre:

Tant que ma main pourra les cordes tendre
Du mignart Lut, pour tes graces chanter:
Tant que l'esprit se voudra contenter
De ne vouloir rien fors que toy comprendre:

Ie ne souhaitte encore point mourir.
Mais quand mes yeus ie sentiray tarir,
Ma voix cassee, et ma main impuissante,
Et mon esprit en ce mortel seiour
Ne pouvant plus montrer signe d'amante:
Priray la Mort noircir mon plus cler iour.

Baise m'encor, rebaise moy et baise:
Donne m'en un de tes plus savoureus,

If only I could spend with him the rest
Of my short days, but spiteful tongues deny!

If, holding me, he were to say, "Dear Love,
Let's make each other happy," telling me
That the storms that dread Euripus' current move
Could not disjoin us, long as life might be;

If, holding him encircled by my arms
As the tree is by the ivy all embraced,
I were caught up, by envious Death prevented,
I should, while soft I felt his kisses' charms,
And while upon his lips my spirit raced,
Die willingly, more than alive, contented.

───────────────

As long as my eyes are able to shed tears
To mourn the passing of my joy with you,
As long as my voice can manage to get through
Its sobs and sighs at all to reach your ears,

As long as my hand can touch the tender strings
Of my dainty lute, to sing aloud your praises,
As long as my soul can concentrate its gazes
On you alone, wishing no other things—

So long I shall not be content to die.
But when I feel my eyes begin to fade,
My voice declined, my hand without its power,
And when my spirit in its mortal stay
Can make no more the signs of love it made,
I'll pray for death to dim my brightest hour.

───────────────

Kiss me again, again, kiss me again!
Give me one of the luscious ones you have,

Donne m'en un de tes plus amoureus:
Je t'en rendray quatre plus chaus que braise.

Las, te plein tu? ça que ce mal j'apaise,
En t'en donnant dix autres doucereus.
Ainsi meslans nos baisers tant heureus
Jouissons nous l'un de l'autre à notre aise.

Lors double vie à chacun en suivra.
Chacun en soy et son ami vivra.
Permets m'Amour penser quelque folie:
Toujours suis mal, vivant discrettement,
Et me ne puis donner contentement
Si hors de moy ne fay quelque saillie.

———————————

Las! que me sert, que si parfaitement
Louas iadis et ma tresse doree,
Et de mes yeus la beauté comparee
A deus Soleils, dont Amour finement

Tira les trets causez de ton tourment?
Ou estes vous, pleurs de peu de duree?
Et Mort par qui deuoit estre honoree
Ta ferme amour et iteré serment?

Donques c'estoit le but de ta malice
De m'asservir sous ombre de service?
Pardonne moy, Amy, à cette fois,
Estant outree et de despite et d'ire:
Mais ie m'assure, quelque part que tu sois,
Qu'autant que moy tu soufres de martire.

———————————

Ne reprenez, Dames, si i'ay aymé:
Si i'ay senti mile torches ardantes,
Mile travaus, mile douleurs mordantes:
Si en pleurant i'ay mon tems consumé,

Give me one of the loving ones I crave:
Four hotter than burning coals I shall return.

What, are you moaning? Let me soothe the pain,
Giving you now ten kisses more, but sweetly;
Thus, our happy kisses joining meetly,
Let us enjoy each other to our gain.

A double life for each of us ensues.
Each in the self and in the lover lives.
Allow me, Love, to feign a pleasing folly:
Living as one, I'm always ill at ease,
And sweet content within me never thrives
Unless outside myself I sometimes sally.

———————————

Alas, what boots it that not long ago
You praised with such finesse my golden hair,
And the beauty of my eyes chose to compare
To double Suns, whence Love allowed to grow

Those features which are cause of all your woe?
Where are you, tears of short duration? Where
The Death that should give evidence most rare
Of your constant love confirmed by solemn vow?

Did this your malice have no other goal
Than to enslave me, feigning to be my slave?
Forgive me, Darling, I'm half out of my mind,
With bitter pain and anger in my soul:
But I tell myself, wherever you may rove,
You feel an anguish of the selfsame kind.

———————————

Do not reproach me, Ladies, if I've loved:
If I have felt a thousand burning arrows,
A thousand pains, a thousand biting sorrows,
If I to constant weeping have been moved,

Las que mon nom n'en soit par vous blamé.
Si i'ay failli, les peines sont presentes,
N'aigrissez point leurs pointes violentes:
Mais estimez qu'Amour, à point nommé,

Sans votre ardeur d'un Vulcan excuser,
Sans la beauté d'Adonis acuser,
Pourra, s'il veut, plus vous rendre amoureuses:
En ayant moins que moi d'ocasion,
Et plus d'estrange et forte passion.
Et gardez vous d'estre plus malheureuses.

Elégie II

D'un tel vouloir le serf point ne desire
La liberté, ou son port le navire,
Comme j'attends, helas, de jour en jour
De toy, Ami, le gracieus retour.
Là, j'avais mis le but de ma douleur,
Qui finirait, quand j'aurais ce bon heur
De te revoir: mais de la longue atente,
Helas, en vain mon desir se lamente.
Cruel, cruel, qui te faisait promettre
Ton brief retour en ta premiere lettre?
As tu si peu de memoire de moy,
Que de m'avoir si tot rompu la foy?
Comme oses tu ainsi abuser celle
Qui de tout tems t'a esté si fidelle?
Or' que tu es aupres de ce rivage
Du Pau cornu, peut estre ton courage
S'est embrasé d'une nouvelle flame,
En me changeant pour prendre une autre Dame:
Ja en oubli inconstamment est mise
La loyauté que tu m'avais promise.
S'il est ainsi, et que desja la foy
Et la bonté se retirent de toy:
Il ne me faut emerveiller si ores
Toute pitié tu as perdu encores.
O combien ha de pensee et de creinte,

Alas, let not your judgment scorn my name.
If I have erred, the punishments I feel;
Don't sharpen any more their pointed steel,
But judge that Love can do to you the same;

Not needing Vulcan to excuse your passion,
Nor the beauty of Adonis its strange fashion,
Love can, when he wishes, make you fall in love;
With less good reason for your fall than mine,
To a stronger, stranger passion you'll incline.
Beware lest greater misery you prove.

Elegy II

No serf could more his liberty desire,
No ship more fervently toward port aspire,
Than I await, alas, from day to day
The news, my love, of your return to me.
My sorrows have that as their only end,
To be achieved at length when I shall bend
My happy eyes on you; but in this waiting,
Desire, alas, complains without abating.
Cruel one, what led you first to write
That I safely might your prompt return await?
Am I so seldom in your memory,
That you so soon have broken faith with me?
How could you dare abuse a lady who
Has been at all times unto you so true?
Perhaps, now that you choose to play a part
Beside the hornèd Po, your changeful heart
Has felt itself inflamed by a new fire
For another lady, goal of your desire:
And in forgetfulness you've filed away
The faith you promised me another day.
If it is so, and if the vows you swore,
And virtue too, reside in you no more,
I need not wonder if it seems that you,
Along with them, have lost all pity too.
How many thoughts, how many fears, oppress,

Tout à par soy, l'ame d'Amour ateinte!
Ores je croy, vu notre amour passee,
Qu'impossible est, que tu m'aies laissee:
Et de nouvel ta foy je me fiance,
Et plus qu'humeine estime ta constance.
Tu es, peut estre, en chemin inconnu
Outre ton gré malade retenu.
Je croy que non: car tant suis coutumiere
De faire aux Dieus pour ta santé priere,
Que plus cruels que tigres ils seroient,
Quand maladie ils te prochasseroient:
Bien que ta fole et volage inconstance
Meriteroit avoir quelque soufrance.
Telle est ma foy, qu'elle pourra sufire
A te garder d'avoir mal et martire.
Celui qui tient au hault Ciel son Empire
Ne me sauroit, ce me semble, desdire:
Mais quand mes pleurs et larmes entendrait
Pour toy prians, son ire il retiendrait.
J'ay de tout tems vescu en son service,
Sans me sentir coulpable d'autre vice
Que de t'avoir bien souvent en son lieu
D'amour forcé, adoré comme Dieu.
Desja deus fois depuis le promis terme
De ton retour, Phebe ses cornes ferme,
Sans que de bonne ou mauvaise fortune
De toy, Ami, J'aye nouvele aucune.
Si toutefois, pour estre enamouré
En autre lieu, tu as tant demouré,
Si say je bien que t'amie nouvelle
A peine aura le renom d'estre telle,
Soit en beauté, vertu, grace et faconde,
Comme plusieurs gens savans par le monde
M'ont fait à tort, ce croy je, estre estimee.
Mais qui pourra garder la renommee?
Non seulement en France suis flatee,
Et beaucoup plus, que ne veus, exaltee.
La terre aussi que Calpe et Pyrenee
Avec la mer tiennent environnee,
Du large Rhin les roulantes areines,
Le beau païs auquel or' te promeines
Ont entendu (tu me l'as fait à croire)
Que gens d'esprit me donnent quelque gloire.

Each in its turn, the soul in love's distress!
Now I believe, in thinking of our love,
It cannot be that you'd unfaithful prove,
And once again I trust your loyalty,
And more than human deem your constancy.
Perhaps you are retained against your will
In some untraveled path, have fallen ill.
I cannot think so, for I daily pray
To the Gods to keep you healthy on your way,
And far more cruel than tigers would they be,
Were they to send to you some malady,
Although your mad inconstancy, indeed,
Might merit that some suffering be your meed.
My faith is such that it can never fail
To guard you from all ill that may assail;
And He Who rules the Empire of the sky
Will not, I think, my fervent pleas deny;
But when He hears these tears and sighs of mine
On your behalf, His wrath He will restrain.
His service have I long been faithful in,
And have been guilty of no other sin
Than having loved you so that, forced by love,
I've adored you in the place of God above.
Two times already since your vowed return
Phoebe in waxing full has closed her horn,
And I've not heard a single word to tell
Whether the fate you've met is good or ill.
At any rate, if you've prolonged your stay
In other lands because along the way
You've found another love, one thing is plain:
She cannot have the fame I know is mine,
For beauty, virtue, eloquence, and grace;
Such am I esteemed, such is the place
That learnèd people—wrongly, in my view—
Do grant me, but who can refuse what's due?
Not just in France am I exalted high,
And, more than I would wish, praised to the sky:
The land that lies between the Pyrenees
And Gibraltar and the sea has heard my praise,
And the shifting sands along the broad-banked Rhine,
And that fair country where you now remain—
They all have heard (and you have told me so)
The glory granted me by those who know.

Goute la bien que tant d'hommes desirent:
Demeure au but ou tant d'autres aspirent:
Et croy qu'ailleurs n'en auras une telle.
Je ne dy pas qu'elle ne soit plus belle:
Mais que jamais femme ne t'aymera,
Ne plus que moy d'honneur te portera.
Maints grans Signeurs à mon amour pretendent,
Et à me plaire et servir prets se rendent,
Joutes et jeus, maintes belles devises
En ma faveur sont par eus entreprises:
Et neanmoins tant peu je m'en soucie,
Que seulement ne les en remercie:
Tu es tout seul, tout mon mal et mon bien:
Avec toy tout, en sans toy je n'ay rien:
Et n'ayant rien qui plaise à ma pensee,
De tout plaisir me treuve delaissee,
Et pour plaisir, ennui saisir me vient.
Le regretter et plorer me convient,
Et sur ce point entre en tel desconfort,
Que mile fois je souhaite la mort.
Ainsi, Ami, ton absence lointeine
Depuis deus mois me tient en cette peine,
Ne vivant pas, mais mourant d'un Amour
Lequel m'occit dix mile fois le jour.
Revien donq tot, si tu as quelque envie
De me revoir encor' un coup en vie.
Et si la mort avant ton arrivee
Ha de mon corps l'aymante ame privee,
Au moins un jour vien, habillé de deuil,
Environner le tour de mon cercueil.
Que plust á Dieu que lors fussent trouvez
Ces quatre vers en blanc marbre engravez.
PAR TOI, AMI, TANT VESQUI ENFLAMMEE,
QU'EN LANGUISSANT PAR FEU SUIS CONSUMEE
QUI COUVE ENCOR SOUS MA CENDRE EMBRAZEE,
SI NE LA RENS DE TES PLEUS APAIZEE.

_____

Enjoy the good so many men desire!
Rest in the goal to which they all aspire!
And know that such a one you won't espy.
Perhaps she's prettier—I'd not deny—
But no woman in the world could love you so,
Or so much honor as I give bestow.
Many great lords to win my love aspire,
And in my service do not seem to tire;
Jousts, devices, many a pretty game
They undertake, and always in my name:
But I, such slight attention do I pay,
I bother not the slightest thanks to say.
You alone my good and evil are:
With you I'm rich, without you I am poor;
And since my thoughts provide nothing to please me,
In pleasure's place comes sorrow then to seize me.
I find that every pleasure's reft from me;
Regret and tears become my destiny,
And thus I plunge into such deep distress,
That a thousand times I've wished for death's release.
And thus, my love, since absent you remain,
For two months now I've languished in this pain—
Living, no, but dying of Love, whose way
It is to kill me ten thousand times a day.
Return then soon, if you an interest have
In seeing me in any sense alive.
And if death, before you ever reach your goal,
Has deprived my body of its loving soul,
Then come one day at least, in mourning clad,
To walk about the tomb where I am laid.
And may God grant that there be not removed
These verses four in marble white engraved:
For you, my love, I lived in such desire
That, languishing, I've been consumed by fire,
Which still will smoulder underneath my clay
Unless your tears will its distress allay.

Elégie III

Quand vous lirez, ô Dames Lionnoises,
Ces miens escrits pleins d'amoureuses noises,
Quand mes regrets, ennuis, despits et larmes
M'orrez chanter en pitoyables carmes,
Ne veuillez pas condamner ma simplesse,
Et jeune erreur de ma fole jeunesse,
Si c'est erreur: mais qui dessous les Cieus
Se peut vanter de n'estre vicieus?
L'un n'est content de sa sorte de vie,
Et toujours porte à ses voisins envie:
L'un forcenant de voir la paix en terre,
Par tous moyens tache y mettre la guerre:
L'autre croyant povreté estre vice,
A autre Dieu qu'or ne fait sacrifice:
L'autre sa foy pariure il emploira
A decevoir quelcun qui le croira:
L'un en mentant de sa langue lezarde,
Mile brocars sur l'un et l'autre darde:
Je ne suis point sous ces planettes nee,
Qui m'ussent pù tant faire infortunee.
Onques ne fut mon oeil marri, de voir
Chez mon voisin mieus que chez moy pleuvoir.
Onq ne mis noise ou discord entre amis:
A faire gain jamais ne me soumis.
Mentir, tromper, et abuser autrui,
Tant m'a desplu, que mesdire de lui.
Mais si en moy rien y ha d'imparfait,
Qu'on blame Amour: c'est lui seul qui l'a fait.
Sur mon verd aage en ses laqs il me prit,
Lors qu'exerçois mon corps et mon esprit
En mile et mile euvres ingenieuses,
Qu'en peu de tems me rendit ennuieuses.
Pour bien savoir avec l'esguille peindre
J'eusse entrepris la renommee esteindre
De celle là, qui plus docte que sage,
Avec Pallas compariot son ouvrage.
Qui m'ust vù lors en armes fiere aller,
Porter la lance et bois faire voler,
Le devoir faire en l'estour furieus,
Piquer, volter le cheval glorieus,
Pour Bradamente, ou la haute Marphise,

Elegy III

When you read, O ladies of Lyon,
These things I've written, full of loving moan,
When you have heard me sing in mournful chants
Of my sorrows, losses, tears, and vain laments,
Don't hasten to condemn me as naive,
Or blame my youth for error, or believe
That error it must be; beneath the sun,
Can any boast that he is such a one
As not to have a vice? One, malcontent,
On envying his neighbor is intent;
Another, peeved to see peace everywhere,
Finds every way he can of starting war;
A third believes that poverty's a vice,
And makes to Gold, not God, his sacrifice;
Another practices his perjuries
To make a fool of everyone he sees;
Another, darting forth his lizard tongue,
Slanders each living soul who comes along.
I wasn't born beneath such stars as those,
Which might have made me wretched and morose.
My eye was never jaundiced once to see
My neighbor showered with gifts not given me.
I never started trouble between friends,
Nor sought, to make a fortune, sordid ends.
To trick, deceive, or make people my prey
Was as alien to me as untruth to say.
But if I have a blemish to my name,
Consider Love; it's he who bears the blame.
When I was young and green he set his snares;
I exercised, in a thousand charming cares,
Both soul and body, but he knew the way
To turn my pastimes into senseless play.
My skill in needle-working was so great
I would have undertaken to compete
With that luckless lady, skillful more than wise,
Who challenged Pallas with her enterprise.
He who had seen me proudly ride to war,
Couch my lance, take on the furious jar
Of combat armed, strike, urge my glorious mount,
Might well have taken me for Bradamant,
Ruggiero's love, or for Marfisa bold,

47

Seur de Roger, il m'ust, possible, prise.
Mais quoy? Amour ne peut longuement voir
Mon coeur n'aymant que Mars et le savoir:
Et me voulant donner autre souci,
En souriant, il me disoit ainsi:
Tu penses donq, ô Lionnoise Dame,
Pouvoir fuir par ce moyen ma flame:
Mais non feras, j'ay subjugué les Dieus
Es bas Enfers, en la Mer et es Cieus.
Et penses tu que n'aye tel pouvoir
Sur les humeins, de leur faire savoir
Qu'il n'y ha rien qui de ma main eschape?
Plus fort se pense et plus tot je le frape.
De me blamer quelquefois tu n'as honte,
En te fiant en Mars, dont tu fais conte:
Mais meintenant, voy si pour persister
En le suivant me pourras resister.
Ainsi parloit. Et tout eschaufé d'ire
Hors de sa trousse une sagette il tire,
Et decochant de son extreme force,
Droit la tira contre ma tendre escorce:
Foible harnois, pour bien couvrir le coeur,
Contre l'Archer qui tousjours est vainqueur.
La bresche faite, entre Amour en la place,
Dont le repos premierement il chasse:
Et de travail qui me donne sans cesse,
Boire, manger, et dormir ne me laisse.
Il ne me chaut de soleil ne d'ombrage:
Je n'ay qu'Amour et feu en mon courage,
Qui me desguise, et fait autre paroitre,
Tant que ne peu moymesme me connoitre.
Je n'avois vù encore seize Hivers,
Lors que j'entray en ces ennuis divers:
Et jà voici le treizième esté
Que mon coeur fut par amour arreté.
Le tems met fin aus hautes Pyramides,
Le tems met fin auts fonteines humides:
Il ne pardonne aus braves Colisees,
Il met à fin les viles plus prisees,
Finir aussi il ha acoutumé
Le feu d'Amour tant soit il allumé:
Mais, las! en moy il semble qu'il augmente
Avec le tems, et que plus me tourmente.

Such martial virtue did I then uphold.
What use? The God of Love was irritated
To see my heart to books and Mars devoted;
Determining to give me other cares,
Smiling he said, "Do you think that, with these airs,
You'll flee my flames, O lady of Lyon?
You won't succeed; my yoke has pressed upon
The Gods themselves, on seas and in the sky
And in the underworld; you can't deny
That I have might to such a high degree
All mortals must admit my mastery
And that nothing in the world escapes my hands.
The most secure falls soonest in my bands.
You have not scrupled to offend my name,
Trusting in Mars, to whom you give all fame;
But now just see: persist within his train,
If so you will, resisting me is vain."
Thus he spoke, and all aflame with ire,
He took an arrow from his copious store
And shot it at me, and I felt the dart
Pierce my tender skin and strike my heart
—Poorly guarded by such feeble mail
Against the Archer who always must prevail.
When the wound was made, Love forthwith took his place
And all tranquillity from me did chase;
And the pain that he bestows forbids me quite
To eat or drink by day or sleep by night.
Sun gives no warmth, nor shadow any rest;
I've only love and fire in my breast,
Which so transform me, working such disguise,
That I myself can scarcely recognize.
I hadn't yet seen sixteen winters pass
When I fell into this manifold distress;
And now my thirtieth summer is at hand,
And my heart remains still under Love's command.
Time crumbles pyramids, however high,
Time in the end makes fountains dead and dry.
It shows no mercy to grand monuments,
Nor at the fall of cities it relents.
It has the custom also, as we know,
Of quenching love as soon as it's aglow.
But alas! In me it seems love is augmented
By time itself; each day I'm more tormented.

Paris ayma Oenone ardamment,
Mais son amour ne dura longuement,
Medee fut aymee de Jason,
Qui tot apres la mit hors sa maison.
Si meritoient elles estre estimees,
Et pour aymer leurs Amis, estre aymees.
S'estant aymé on peut Amour laisser
N'est il raison, ne l'estant, se lasser?
N'est il raison te prier de permettre,
Amour, que puisse à mes tourmens fin mettre?
Ne permets point que de Mort face espreuve,
Et plus que toy pitoyable la treuve:
Mais si tu veus que j'ayme jusqu'au bout,
Fay que celui que j'estime mon tout,
Que seul me peut faire plorer et rire,
Et pour lequel si souvent je soupire,
Sente en ses os, en son sang, en son ame,
Ou plus ardente, ou bien esgale flame.
Alors ton faix plus aisé me sera,
Quand avec moy quelcun le portera.

With fervent ardor Paris gave his love
To Oenone, but his passion brief did prove;
Medea's art did Jason's love arouse,
But very soon he drove her from his house.
These women loved their men enough to earn,
Surely, that they should be loved in return.
If, being loved, some can that love disdain,
Why can't rejected lovers shun their pain?
Is it not just that, unloved, I should flee?
Not just that I should beg you to agree,
Love, that my torments finally should cease?
Don't force me to seek Death to find release,
And see her more than you a pitying friend.
But if you insist I love right to the end,
Bring it about that he who is my all,
Who makes me weep or laugh as at his call,
May feel within his bones, his blood, his soul,
A fire like mine, or worse, consume him whole.
Your burden will be easier to bear,
When another has to hold with me his share.

Gaspara Stampa

Gaspara Stampa
(1524?—1554)

Although born in Padua, Gaspara Stampa moved with her family to
Venice when she was still a child, and there she spent the remainder of
her short life. Generally regarded as the greatest woman poet of the
Italian Renaissance, she provides, in both her life and work, a dramatic
contrast with the other close contender for that honor, Vittoria Colonna,
great aristocrat and Platonic beloved of Michelangelo. Vittoria was noble,
Gaspara bourgeoise; Vittoria was Roman, Gaspara Venetian; Vittoria was
a wife and chatelaine, Gaspara a prostitute; Vittoria's poems embody the
highest ideals of Christian and Platonic virtue, Gaspara's poems—if we
except the relatively small number of poems of Christian repentance
with which her *canzoniere* closes—are devoted exclusively to obsessive
sexual love, particularly to the torments of its frustration.

It is misleading to identify Gaspara Stampa simply as a prostitute. She
was, as the Introduction has already indicated, a *cortigiana onesta* or
"honest courtesan," and as such enjoyed a social status of some dignity.
We know little about her life, and most of what we know comes from her
poetry. From some contemporary references we glean a little more
information. Her father, a jeweler and hence a member of the artisan
class, died while she was still a girl; the next we hear of her, as a young
woman, she is, together with her brother Baldassare and her sister
Cassandra, an artistic ornament of Venetian society. Baldassare was a
poet (some of his work survives), Cassandra was a singer, and Gaspara
was both poet and singer. We would be misled, however, if we were to
picture these activities in twentieth-century terms. Cassandra would not
be in a position to get a try out at the Met or a role in a Broadway
musical, any more than Baldassare would be likely to be offered a job as
poet-in-residence at a university. They belonged, clearly, to the Venetian

demimonde—artistic talent was a part of their entrée into that world, a world populated by aristocrats, by high dignitaries of church and state. Music and poetry were not the only activities pursued in that world.

Venice in the sixteenth century was a city remarkable for its prosperity, its sophistication, its love of luxury and pleasure, and its notable indifference to the more rigorous moral prescriptions of Christianity. It was a city of art and sensuality, and the links between the two were close. Sexuality was one of the pleasures most strenuously pursued by the Venetian upper classes (even the common whores of Venice were famous throughout Europe for their beauty), but the more refined among them expected an ambience where sexuality was fused with art. Hence, I believe, the artistic attainments of the Stampa siblings. Art and sexuality together explain their presence in this social milieu. What else, one might ask, would give the bourgeois trio access to that milieu?

As I have already observed, Gaspara's position as a *cortigiana onesta*, far from subjecting her to opprobrium, assured for her a certain degree of esteem. The complimentary poems praising her beauty and her artistic gifts seem full of sincere admiration—even if they do betray at times, the same faint leer that similar poems in praise of Louise Labé exhibit (and Abdelkader Salza, in his edition of Gaspara, reprints a scurrilous contemporaneous epitaph taxing her with sexual vice).[1] It might well occur that a young Venetian male of privileged class, powerful and respected, would establish a liaison with such a woman—not marriage, to be sure, but nevertheless a liaison of some solidity, mutual respect, and duration.

Count Collaltino di Collalto was the lover and protector of Gaspara Stampa. On the evidence of her poems, he found her attractive enough to be worth his time, and attractive—or importunate—enough to elicit from him vows of eternal love and fidelity. On the same evidence, he was the transfiguring love of Gaspara's life—not her first lover, it would seem, nor yet her last, and yet her only true love. However obsessive love may have been for Gaspara—and on the basis of the poems she either was indeed possessed or was one of the greatest fiction writers of all time—it was not obsessive for Collaltino. For him, apparently, sex was fine in its place, but it was nowhere near as interesting as war. He entered the service of Henri II of France, who was at that time busy with a number of campaigns, and departed, promising to write. He didn't write . . .

> Hast du der Gaspara Stampa
> denn genügend gedacht, dass irgend ein Mädchen,
> dem der Geliebte entging, am gesteigerten Beispiel
> dieser Liebenden fühlt: dass ich würde wie sie?

54

Sollen nicht endlich uns diese ältesten Schmerzen
fruchtbarer werden? Ist es nicht Zeit, dass wir liebend
uns vom Geliebten befrein und es bebend bestehn:
wie der Pfeil die Sehne besteht, um gesammelt im Absprung
mehr zu sein als er selbst. Denn Bleiben ist nirgends.[2]

> Have you thought of her enough.
> Of Gaspara Stampa, and that any girl
> Whose lover has left her might feel that exalted example
> Of that loving woman, and might feel: "May I be like her?"
> Isn't it finally time for these oldest of sorrows
> To become more fruitful for us? Isn't it time
> That we, loving, free ourselves from the beloved,
> And endure it, trembling, as the arrow endures the bow,
> That, collected in its leaping, it may be
> *More* than itself. For staying is no place.

(translated by F. J. Warnke)

So wrote Rainer Maria Rilke in the first of his *Duino Elegies* (1912/1922).
The figure of Gaspara Stampa, like that of Louise Labé, was of enormous
importance for the great German poet. Elsewhere, in his *Aufzeichnungen
des Malte Laurids Brigge,* he refers again to Gaspara, and to Louise Labé
(as well as Héloïse, the Comtesse de Die, Clara d'Anduze, and others). It
is the passage in which he draws a distinction between the *Geliebte* and
the *Liebende*—between the "beloved" and the "loving one": the *Geliebte*
"lives poorly, and always in danger"; the *Liebende* is surrounded by "the
most complete certainty." The "loving ones" "fling themselves after the
lost one, but with the very first step they overtake him, and *in front of*
them is only God."[3]

The woman love poet is, then, for Rilke, a crucial figure of the love
that, transcending itself and any ego, becomes divine. To what extent is
this a valid perception, or to what extent Rilke's projection of his own
creation? In the case of Gaspara Stampa, at least, it seems that Rilke has
commented on what is truly in the text. For, as I've suggested in the
Introduction, Gaspara has learned what Socrates taught to Phaedrus,
what Mann's Aschenbach calls "perhaps the tenderest, most mocking
thought that ever was thought"—that the lover is nearer the divine than
is the beloved.[4] Even in the early part of her *canzoniere*, before the
abandonment, Gaspara's hyperbolic praises of Collaltino's superiority
(e.g., "Le doti preclare di lui furono le sue dolci catene") are interspersed
with poems which, as Vitiello notes, assert the moral superiority con-
ferred upon her by her pure love.[5]

There is much Petrarch in Gaspara, as there is in virtually all sixteenth-century love lyrists. The first of her sonnets, for example, is a pastiche of the first of Petrarch's *Rime,* and the second tells how she first saw Collaltino near Christmas, as Petrarch first saw Laura on Good Friday. The most important of her modifications of Petrarchism is her insistence on the motif of the love which elevates the lover above the beloved. The sonnet beginning "Se, cosí come sono abietta e vile/donna" will perhaps make that point as well as any other:

> Se, cosí come sono abietta e vile
> donna, posso portar sí alto foco,
> perché non debbo aver almeno un poco
> di ritraggerlo al mondo e vena e stile?
>
> S'Amor con novo, insolito focile,
> ov'io non potea gir, m'alzò a tal loco,
> perché non può non con usato gioco
> far la pena e la penna in me simile?
>
> E, se non può per forza di natura,
> puollo almen per miracolo, che spesso
> vince, trapassa e rompe ogni misura.
> Come ciò sia non posso dir espresso;
> io provo ben che per mia gran ventura
> mi sento il cor di novo stile impresso.

> If, being a woman so abject and vile,
> I nonetheless can bear so high a flame,
> Why should I not give to the world the same,
> At least in part, in proper wealth and style?
>
> If Love, with a new, unprecedented spark,
> Could raise me to a place I could not reach,
> Why cannot pain and pen combine to teach
> Such arts as, never known, shall find their mark?
>
> And if this does not lie in Nature's art,
> Then let it be by miracle, whose power
> Can conquer, transcend, and every limit break.
> How this may be I cannot say for sure,
> But well I know the fortune I partake,
> And through it a new style engraves my heart.

It is not Collaltino who has made of Gaspara a poet; it is rather her "flame," the love she bears for him. Gaspara is her own Muse as, according to Graves, Sor Juana was hers.

Art is but one of Gaspara's themes, however, and it would give a false impression of her lyric achievement if one were to imply that the entire *canzoniere* is neatly dominated by that theme. Indeed, the very variety, inconsistency, and contradiction implicit in the sequence bestow upon it its quality as a singularly accurate account of the turmoil of sexual love. In "Ella un dì sarà libera; egli, tardi, pentito," she shifts focus inexplicably, referring to her absent lover in the third person in the initial quatrain, then shifting to a direct address in which she predicts with sadistic glee the sorrows he will one day feel when he repents his cruelty. In "Io non v'invidio punto, angeli santi," she compares her joy in seeing Collaltino with the joy felt by the angels on beholding the face of God:

> Holy angels, I don't envy you
> For all your glory and your bliss above,
> And those desires that, filled, arouse still love,
> You who have always highest God in view:
>
> For my delights are such, and of such measure
> That earthly hearts can't comprehend their size,
> As long as I can see those candid eyes,
> And justly sing and celebrate my treasure.
>
> Just as your thirst is slaked for you in Heaven
> By gazing always on His face divine,
> Down here the infinite to me is given
> As long as I can know my lover's mine.
> In this alone your joy wins, to my sorrow:
> Yours last forever; mine could end tomorrow.

In "Per le saette tue, Amore, ti giuro" she expresses her fear, not of the pains of love, but rather of the possibility of their cessation. In "O gran valor d'un cavalier cortese" she rages ironically at her absent lover, reminding him that his royal master, Henri II, does not scorn to follow Venus as well as Mars:

> O great exploit of gentle cavalier:
> To have carried off to France with him the heart
> Of a rash young girl whom Love did from the start
> Subdue when the splendor of his eyes came near!

57

At least if you had kept your promise keen
To salve my grief with one or two brief letters!
But you, my Lord, are one who chiefly betters
His honor, and all other vows are vain.

But in the ancient chronicles I've read
That the greatest heroes did not find it shame
To follow jointly Mars and Venus fair.
And of the King, your master, it is said
Both love and war impose an equal claim,
Whence he is famed from east to western shore.

Another sonnet, "Rimandatemi il cor, empio tiranno," is interesting
not only as an amorous complaint but also for its identification of
Collaltino as her one-time protector:

Send back my heart to me, relentless one,
Who, tyrantlike, do hold and tear it so,
And do to it, and me, just what is done
By tigers and lions to the hapless doe.

Eight days have passed, at least a year to me;
No messages, no letters, do I get,
Despite the vows with which you were so free:
Fountain of valor, Count, and of deceit!

Am I Hercules or Samson, do you suppose,
To bear such sorrow now that we're apart?
I'm young, a woman, half out of my mind,
And, most of all, I'm here without my heart,
You being gone, in whom I used to find
Defense, who were for me strength and repose.

Venice plays a specific role in Gaspara's poetry, both as theme and as
setting. Her "Elegiac Lament" in terza rima locates the poet specifically
in that city on "the rich and blessed Adriatic shores" which is the "nest of
love and nest of courtesy," and the sonnet "Io son da l'aspettar omai sí
stanca" draws a vivid contrast between the waves of the maritime city—
the element, as it were, of the female lover—and the inland hills on
which the unfaithful Collaltino enjoys his martial sport:

Io son da l'aspettar omai sí stanca,
sí vinta dal dolor e dal disio,

per la sí poca fede e molto oblio
di chi del suo tornar, lassa, mi manca,

che lei, che'l mondo impalidisce e 'mbianca
con la sua falce e dà l'ultimo fio,
chiamo talor per refrigerio mio,
sí 'l dolor nel mio petto si rinfranca.

Ed ella si fa sorda al mio chiamare,
schernendo i miei pensier fallaci e folli,
come sta sordo anch'egli al suo tornare.
Cosí col pianto, ond'ho gli occhi miei molli,
fo pietose quest'onde e questo mare;
ed ei si vive lieto ne' suoi colli.

By now this waiting has so wearied me
So vanquished am I by desire and grief
For him who, absent, grants me no relief,
So faithless, so forgetful, still is he,

That I turn and beg that she will give me ease,
Who with her sickle makes the world turn white
And gives to all the final blow; my plight
Such sorrow wrings from me, such anguished pleas.

But she is deaf to this my wretched crying,
And scorns my scattered thoughts disturbed and vain,
Like him who, deaf to me, grants no replying.
Thus with lament that from my eyes distills
I wake the pity of these waves, this main,
While he, lighthearted, lives among his hills.

It's a rather complex poem. The female deity evoked in the second quatrain is clearly the moon, but she is equally clearly Death. The double identity is explained if we remember that the moon is Diana, who has a triple identity as maiden, nymph, and crone. In her aspect as crone she is also Hecate, goddess of the underworld and hence associated with death. Diana is also, of course, the goddess of chastity, and her spurning of the poet's plea can be construed as punishment for the poet's betrayal in having given herself over to love. Gaspara's poems often have this kind of complexity of reverberation.

Finally Gaspara got tired of waiting and took another lover (as her later poems imply). Probably more than one. These later experiences did not, however, trigger the intense emotion that Collalto had evoked. Artistic expression comparable to that of the Collalto poems appears only in the poems of repentance with which the *canzoniere* ends.

The heiress of a great, complex, and highly sophisticated lyric tradition, Gaspara Stampa was capable of modifying it in such a way as to make it expressive of a female situation and sensibility. In so doing, she brought it once more to life. For she stands out like a beacon amid the masses of Petrarchan lyrists of the *cinquecento*. Dealing with the materials and conventions of the tradition, she imbued them with immediacy and sincerity—or with the illusion of those qualities, which is, in art, the same thing. Among her immediate contemporaries, only Michelangelo was able to do more; among her immediate successors, only Tasso. And, in the sixteenth century, perhaps only these three Italian lyrists are worthy of their master, Petrarch.

NOTES

1. Gaspara Stampa/Veronica Franco, *Rime,* ed. A. Salza (Bari, 1913), p. 196.
2. R. M. Rilke, *Werke,* ed. B. Allemann, 3 vols. (Frankfurt-am-Main, 1966), 1:442–43.
3. Ibid., 3:324.
4. Thomas Mann, "Death in Venice," in *Death in Venice and Other Stories,* trans. H. T. Lowe-Porter (New York, Knopf, 1954), pp. 45–46.
5. J. Vitiello, "Gaspara Stampa: The Ambiguities of Martyrdom," *MLN* 90 (1975): 58–71.

Il primo giorno del suo amore

Era vicino il dí che 'l Creatore,
che ne l'altezza sua potea restarsi,
in forma umana venne a dimostrarsi,
dal ventre virginal uscendo fore,

quando degnò l'illustre mio signore,
per cui ho tanti poi lamenti sparsi,
potendo in luogo piú alto annidarsi,
farsi nido e ricetto del mio core.

Ond'io sí rara e sí alta ventura
accolsi lieta; e duolmi sol che tardi
mi fe' degna di lei l'eterna cura.
Da indi in qua pensieri e speme e sguardi
volsi a lui tutti, fuor d'ogni misura
chiaro e gentil, quanto 'l sol giri e guardi.

―――――――――

Le doti preclare di lui furono le sue dolci catene

Un intelletto angelico e divino,
una real natura ed una valore,
un disio vago di fama e d'onore,
un parlar saggio, grave e pellegrino,

un sangue illustre, agli alti re vicino,
una fortuna a poche altre minore,
un'etá nel suo proprio e vero fiore,
un atto onesto, mansueto e chino,

un viso piú che 'l sol lucente e chiaro,
ove bellezza e grazia Amor riserra
in non mai piú vedute o udite tempre,
fûr le catene, che giá mi legâro,
e mi fan dolce ed onorata guerra.
O pur piaccia ad Amor che stringan sempre!

―――――――――

The first day of her love

The day approached when He Who created all,
And Who, had He willed, could have remained on high,
In human form in virgin womb did lie,
Thence issuing, Himself full to reveal,

When my own noble lord, who might have chosen
More lofty station, deigned to choose my heart
To make his nest, whence I've received such smart
That sighs innumerable from me have risen.

Joyfully I embraced this blessed chance
So rare and so exalted, just regretting
That eternal Providence so late did render
Me worthy of him. Each and every glance,
Each hope and thought of mine to him I tender,
Who is noble as the sun rising or setting.

———————————

His excellent qualities have been her sweet chains

An intellect angelic and divine,
A royal nature, of valorous deeds untiring,
Ardent desire, toward honored fame aspiring,
Sober in speech, and dignified in mien;

Of illustrious blood, to noble kings related,
Possessed of wealth inferior to few,
In the flower of his age and fair to view,
Mild in manner, in courtesy unbated;

A face more clear and radiant than the sun,
Where grace and beauty were by Love bestowed
To a degree that seen or heard was never:
Such are the chains that Love on me does load;
By sweet and honored war I am undone.
O may Love choose in these bonds to hold me ever!

———————————

Amore, che l'ha sollevata a lui, ispira i suoi versi

Se, cosi come sono abietta e vile
donna, posso portar sí alto foco,
perché non debbo aver almeno un poco
di ritraggerlo al mondo e vena e stile?

S'Amor con novo, insolito focile,
ov'io non potea gir, m'alzò a tal loco,
perché non può non con usato gioco
far la pena e la penna in me simile?

E, se non può per forza di natura,
puollo almen per miracolo, che spesso
vince, trapassa e rompe ogni misura.
Come ciò sia non posso dir espresso;
io provo ben che per mia gran ventura
mi sento il cor di novo stile impresso.

————————

Ella un dì sarà libera; egli, tardi, pentito

S'avien ch'un giorno Amor a me mi renda,
e mi ritolga a questo empio signore;
di che paventa, e non vorrebbe, il core,
tal gioia del penar suo par che prenda; ·

voi chiamerete invan la mia stupenda
fede, e l'immenso e smisurato amore,
di vostra crudeltá, di vostro errore
tardi pentito, ove non è chi intenda.

Ed io, cantando la mia libertade,
da cosí duri lacci e crudi sciolta,
passerò lieta a la futura etade.
E, se giusto pregar in ciel s'ascolta,
vedrò forse anco in man di crudeltade
la vita vostra a mia vendetta involta.

————————

Love, having elevated her to him, inspires her verses

If, being a woman so abject and vile,
I nonetheless can bear so high a flame,
Why should I not give to the world the same,
At least in part, in proper wealth and style?

If Love, with a new, unprecedented spark,
Could raise me to a place I could not reach,
Why cannot pain and pen combine to teach
Such arts as, never known, shall find their mark?

And if this does not lie in Nature's art,
Then let it be by miracle, whose power
Can conquer, transcend, and every limit break.
How this may be I cannot say for sure,
But well I know the fortune I partake,
And through it a new style engraves my heart.

————————————

She will be one day free; he, too late, repentant

If one day Love gives back to me my heart
And delivers me from this my impious lord,
My unwilling heart, which terror hath endured,
Such joy he takes in the pain he can impart;

You'll call in vain upon my love unmeasured
And vast, and on my faith so freely given,
Repenting of your cruelty; unshriven
Of all you'll rue the gifts that were untreasured.

While I, my liberty so gaily singing,
Released from bondage harsh and cruel, shall go
With springing step into my future state.
And if the heavens justice do bestow
On earnest prayers, I'll see a cruel hand wait
To seize your life, thus vengeance to me bringing.

————————————

"Io non v'invidio punto, angeli santi . . ."

Io von v'invidio punto, angeli santi,
le vostre tante glorie e tanti beni,
e que' disir di ciò che braman pieni,
stando voi sempre a l'alto Sire avanti;

perché i diletti miei son tali e tanti,
che non posson capire in cor terreni,
mentr'ho davanti i lumi almi e sereni,
di cui conven che sempre scriva e canti.

E come in ciel gran refrigerio e vita
dal volto Suo solete voi fruire,
tal io qua giú da la beltá infinita.
In questo sol vincete il mio gioire,
che la vostra è eterna e stabilita,
e la mia gloria può tosto finire.

———————————

Non teme la pena amorosa, ma la fine di essa

Per le saette tue, Amor, ti giuro,
e per la tua possente e sacra face,
che, se ben questa m'arde e 'l cor mi sface,
e quelle mi feriscon, non mi curo;

quantunque nel passato e nel futuro
qual l'une acute, e qual l'altra vivace,
donne amorose, e prendi qual ti piace,
che sentisser giamai né fian, né fûro;

Perché nasce virtú da questa pena,
che 'l senso del dolor vince ed abbaglia,
sí che o non duole, o non si sente appena.
Quel, che l'anima e 'l corpo mi travaglia,
è la temenza ch'a morir mi mena,
che 'l foco mio non sia foco di paglia.

———————————

"Holy angels, I don't envy you"

Holy angels, I don't envy you
For all your glory and your bliss above,
And those desires that, filled, arouse still love,
You who have always highest God in view:

For my delights are such, and of such measure
That earthly hearts can't comprehend their size,
As long as I can see those candid eyes,
And justly sing and celebrate my treasure.

Just as your thirst is slaked for you in Heaven
By gazing always on His face divine,
Down here the infinite to me is given
As long as I can know my lover's mine.
In this alone your joy wins, to my sorrow:
Yours lasts forever; mine could end tomorrow.

———————————

She does not fear amorous pain, but rather its end

Love, by your mighty arrows thus I swear,
And by the sacred, potent torch you carry:
Though the latter burn me, make my heart its quarry,
And the former wound me, still I do not care;

Delve in the past or in the future gaze,
You'll never find a woman who love's anguish
Could feel as I have, or like me could languish
In the arrows' sharpness, the torch's furious blaze;

For of these pains a special virtue is born,
Which dulls and conquers every sense of sorrow,
So that it doesn't hurt, does scarcely gnaw.
And that, which does both soul and body harrow,
Is the fear that leads me to my death forlorn:
That my fire may prove to be a fire of straw.

———————————

Stanca d'aspettarlo, ella talora invoca la morte

Io son da l'aspettar omai sí stanca,
sí vinta dal dolor e dal disio,
per la sí poca fede e molto oblio
di chi del suo tornar, lassa, mi manca,

   che lei, che 'l mondo impalidisce e 'mbianca
con la sua falce e dà l'ultimo fio,
chiamo talor per refrigerio mio,
sí 'l dolor nel mio petto si rinfranca.

   Ed ella si fa sorda al mio chiamare,
schernendo i miei pensier fallaci e folli,
come sta sordo anch'egli al suo tornare.
   Cosí col pianto, ond'ho gli occhi miei molli,
fo pietose quest'onde e questo mare;
ed ei si vive lieto ne' suoi colli.

   Il cor verrebbe teco,
nel tuo partir, signore,
s'egli fosse piú meco,
poi che con gli occhi tuoi mi prese Amore.
Dunque verranno teco i sospir miei,
che sol mi son restati
fidi compagni e grati,
e le voci e gli omei;
e, se vedi mancarti la lor scorta,
pensa ch'io sarò morta.

Egli, in Francia, ha seco il cuore di lei; e non le scrive

O gran valor d'un cavalier cortese,
d'aver portato fin in Francia il core

"By now this waiting so has wearied me"

By now this waiting so has wearied me,
So vanquished am I by desire and grief
For him who, absent, grants me no relief,
So faithless, so forgetful, still is he,

That I turn and beg that she will give me ease,
Who with her sickle makes the world turn white
And gives to all the final blow; my plight
Such sorrow wrings from me, such anguished pleas.

But she is deaf to this my wretched crying,
And scorns my scattered thoughts disturbed and vain,
Like him who, deaf to me, grants no replying.
Thus with lament that from my eyes distills
I wake the pity of these waves, this main,
While he, lighthearted, lives among his hills.

    With you my heart would rove,
In your voyaging, my Lord,
But a heart I do not have,
Since, with your eyes, Love seized me as his ward.
Thus my sighs will be companions on your way
—My cries and sobbings too,
Comrades fair and true,
The only ones who stay—;
And if you find yourself by them forsaken,
You'll know Death has me taken.

"O great exploit of gentle cavalier"

O great exploit of gentle cavalier:
To have carried off to France with him the heart

d'una giovane incauta, ch'Amore
a lo splendor de' suoi begli occhi prese!

Almen m'aveste le promesse attese
di temprar con due versi il mio dolore,
mentre, signor, a procacciarvi onore
tutte le voglie avete ad una intese.

I' ho pur letto ne l'antiche carte
che non ebber a sdegno i grandi eroi
parimente seguir Venere e Marte.
E del re, che seguite, udito ho poi
che queste cure altamente comparte,
ond' è chiar dagli espèri ai lidi eoi.

————————————

"Son passati otto giorni, a me un anno . . ."

Rimandatemi il cor, empio tiranno,
ch'a sí gran torto avete ed istraziate,
e di lui e di me quel proprio fate,
che le tigri e i leon di cerva fanno.

Son passati otto giorni, a me un anno,
ch'io non ho vostre lettere od imbasciate,
contra le fé che voi m'avete date,
o fonte di valor, conte, e d'inganno.

Credete ch'io sia Ercol o Sansone
a poter sostener tanto dolore,
giovane e donna e fuor d'ogni ragione,
massime essendo qui senza 'l mio core
e senza voi a mia difensione,
onde mi suol venir forza e vigore?

————————————

Of a rash young girl whom Love did from the start
Subdue when the splendor of his eyes came near!

At least if you had kept your promise keen
To salve my grief with one or two brief letters!
But you, my Lord, are one who chiefly betters
His honor, and all other vows are vain.

But in the ancient chronicles I've read
That the greatest heroes did not find it shame
To follow jointly Mars and Venus fair.
And of the King,[1] your master, it is said
Both love and war impose an equal claim,
Whence he is famed from west to eastern shore.

---

1. Henri II, the French king whose service Count Collaltino had entered, was renowned as both a lover and a soldier.

"Send back my heart to me, relentless one"

Send back my heart to me, relentless one,
Who, tyrantlike, do hold and tear it so,
And do to it, and me, just what is done
By tigers and lions to the hapless doe.

Eight days have passed, at least a year to me;
No messages, no letters, do I get,
Despite the vows with which you were so free:
Fountain of valor, Count, and of deceit!

Am I Hercules or Samson, do you suppose,
To bear such sorrow now that we're apart?
I'm young, a woman, half out of my mind,
And, most of all, I'm here without my heart,
You being gone, in whom I used to find
Defense, who were for me strength and repose.

Ad ogni Natale, le torna a mente il primo amore

Io non veggio giamai giunger quel giorno,
ove nacque Colui che carne prese,
essendo Dio, per scancellar l'offese
del nostro padre al suo Fattor ritorno,

che non mi risovenga il modo adorno,
col quale, avendo Amor le reti tese
fra due begli occhi ed un riso, mi prese:
occhi, ch'or fan da me lunge soggiorno;

e de l'antico amor qualche puntura
io non senta al desire ed al cor darmi,
sí fu la piaga mia profonda e dura.
E, se non che ragion pur prende l'armi
e vince il senso, questa acerba cura
sarebbe or tal che non potrebbe aitarmi.

Elegiaco lamento, essendo egli lontano

De le ricche, beate e chiare rive
d'Adria, di cortesia nido e d'Amore,
ove sí dolce si soggiorna e vive,
donna, avendo lontano il suo signore,
quando il sol si diparte, e quando poi
a noi rimena il matutino albore,
per isfogar gli ardenti disir suoi,
con queste voci lo sospira e chiama;
voi, rive, che l'udite, ditel voi.
Tu, che volando vai di rama in rama,
consorte amata e fida tortorella,
e sai quanto si tema e quanto s'ama,
quando, volando in questa parte e n' quella,
sei vicina al mio ben, mostragli aperto
in note, ch'abbian voce di favella:
digli quant'è 'l mio stato aspro ed incerto,
or che, lassa, da lui mi trovo lunge

On every Christmas her first love returns to her mind

I never see return that blessed day,
When He was born, Himself the God of all,
And took on flesh that He might wipe away
Our father's sin against his maker's will,

Without remembering the subtle skill
With which Love caught me, spreading out his net
Between the eyes and smile that haunt me still,
Eyes far away that I cannot forget;

And I cannot help but feel the ancient wound
Which Love gave to my heart and my desires,
So deep that wound was, and so harsh its pain;
Did reason not take up its arms again
To vanquish my senses, these consuming fires
Would be such that no succor could be found.

Elegiac lament, her love being far away

From the rich and blessèd Adriatic shores,
Nest of love and nest of courtesy,
Where sweet it is to live amid allures,
    A lady for her absent lord did cry,
And both at setting sun and at the dawn,
Made sad complaint with many a dismal sigh:
    Tell us, you shores, the burden of her moan:
"Faithful turtle-dove, belovèd spouse,
You who from branch to branch in vain have flown,
    Who know what pains both fear and love arouse,
When you, in flying here and there, come near
To where my love is, sing to him my cause,
    And with your voice of flame approach his ear:
Tell him how bitter my state is, how unsure,
Now that, alas, I find myself so far

73

per ria fortuna mia e non per merto.

E tu, rosignuolin, quando ti punge
giusto disio di disfogar tuoi lai
con voce ove cantando non s'aggiunge,

digli, dolente quanto fossi mai,
che la mia vita è tutta oscura notte,
essendo priva di quei dolci rai.

E tu, che 'n cave e solitarie grotte,
Eco, soggiorni, il suon de'miei lamenti
rendi a l'orecchie sue con voci rotte.

E voi, dolci aure ed amorosi venti,
i miei sospir accolti in lunga schiera
deh fate all signor mio tutti presenti.

E voi, che lunga e dolce primavera
serbate, ombrose selve, e sète spesso
fido soggiorno a questa e a quella fièra,

mostrate tutte al mio signore espresso
che non pur i diletti mi son noia,
ma la vita m'è morte anco senz'esso.

Ei si portò, partendo, ogni mia gioia,
e, se, tornando omai, non la rimena,
per forza converrà tosto ch'io moia.

La speme sola al viver mio dà lena,
la qual, non tornand'ei, non può durare,
da soverchio disio vinta e da pena.

Quell'ore, ch'io solea tutte passare
liete e tranquille, mentre er'ei presente,
or ch'egli è lunge son tornate amare.

Ma, lassa, a torto del suo mal si pente,
a torto chiama il suo destin crudele,
chi volontario al suo morir consente.

Lassa, io devea con mie giuste querele
o far che non andasse, o far ch'andando
non desse al vento senza me le vele;

ch'or non m'andrei dolente lamentando,
né temenza d'oblio, né gelosia
non m'avrebber di me mandata in bando.

Emendate, signor, la colpa mia
voi, ritornando ove 'l vostro ritorno
piú che la propria vita si disia.

E, se rimena il sole un dí quel giorno,
non pensate mai piú da me partire,

From him, and unjust fortune must endure.
And you, sweet nightingale, when you're impelled
To give vent in your lays to longing pure,
　　With a voice whose singing cannot be excelled,
Tell him, complaining with all might and main,
That my life to darkest night has been compelled,
　　Now that without those sweet rays I remain.
And Echo, you who dwell in grot and cave
Alone, take the harsh burden of my pain,
　　And carry to his ears its bitter stave.
And you, sweet airs and zephyrs amorous,
The long procession of my sighs receive
　　And bear them to my lord so generous.
You shady groves, prolonging a sweet spring,
You who often prove felicitous,
　　To many a beast fair refuge offering,
Convey unto my lord, and speedily,
That my delights no pleasure to me bring,
　　And my life is death, since he is not with me.
In leaving he took with him all my joy,
Which without him I nevermore shall see,
　　But shall perforce meet death without delay.
'Tis hope alone gives meaning to my life,
Which boundless desire and endless pain destroy,
　　Should he not return it soon will end its strife.
Those hours which I used to spend in bliss
And peace are now with bitter sorrow rife,
　　Now that I must his dearest presence miss.
But oh, alas, all falsely they complain,
And cruel destiny condemn amiss,
　　Who with free will consent to deadly pain.
Alas, I should with my incessant wails
Have kept him here, or used them to obtain
　　That without me he would not raise his sails;
And thus I would not be lamenting ever,
Nor would the fear that in my heart prevails,
　　This jealous fear, thus from myself me sever.
Correct, my dearest lord, my fault; return
To where your always desolated lover
　　More than for life itself for you does yearn
And if the sun should ever bring that day,
Think nevermore of parting from this bourn,

ch'io non vi sia da presso notte e giorno,
poi ch'io mi veggo senza voi morire.

Spera nel soccorso divino

—Volgi a me, peccatrice empia, la vista—
mi grida il mio Signor che 'n croce pende;
e dal mio cieco senso non s'intende
la voce sua di vera pietà mista,

sí mi trasforma Amor empio e contrista,
e d'altro foco il cor arde ed accende;
sí l'alma al proprio e vero ben contende,
che non si perde mai, poi che s'acquista.

La ragion saria ben facile e pronta
a seguire il suo meglio; ma li svia
questa fral carne, che con lei s'affronta.
Dunque apparir non può la luce mia,
se 'l sol de la tua grazia non sormonta
a squarciar questa nebbia fosca e ria.

"Dolce Signor, non mi lasciar perire!"

Mesta e pentita de' miei gravi errori
e del mio vaneggiar tanto e sí lieve,
e d'aver speso questo tempo breve
de la vita fugace in vani amori,

a te, Signor, ch'intenerisci i cori,
e rendi calda la gelata neve,
e fai soave ogn'aspro peso e greve
a chiunque accendi di tuoi santi ardori,

For I would be beside you night and day;
Without you I see myself within the urn."

She hopes for divine aid

"Impious sinner, turn your face to me,"
My Lord cries out, as on the cross He hangs;
His voice is filled with true compassion's pangs,
But my blind senses do not heed His plea,

So am I by my wretched Love transmuted,
And by such different fire my heart is seared;
Yet is my soul to true delight allured,
Which, once acquired, cannot be disputed.

Reason would follow fain its goal on high
With swift alacrity, but is misguided
By this frail flesh, which ever it opposes.
And thus my light remains from me divided,
Unless the sun of your grace itself imposes,
This dark and evil fog to drive away.

"Sweetest Lord, o do not let me die!"

Sad and repentant for my errors grave,
And the wild delirium that stole my sanity,
And for having spent the few years that I have
Of fleeting life in amorous vanity,

I turn to you, O Lord, who can make tender
The hardest hearts, and warm the coldest snow,
And who the harshest burden sweet can render
For those enkindled by your sacred glow.

ricorro; e prego che mi porghi mano
a trarmi fuor del pelago, onde uscire,
s'io tentassi da me, sarebbe vano.
    Tu volesti per noi, Signor, morire,
tu ricomprasti tutto il seme umano;
dolce Signor, non mi lasciar perire!

———————————

And I pray that you'll extend your hand to me
And pull me from this stormy sea, whence I
Could never rise through efforts of my own.
You died for us, my Lord, you did atone,
Paying for all the human race the fee.
Sweetest Lord, O do not let me die!

———————

Sor Juana Inés de la Cruz

Sor Juana Inés de la Cruz (1648–1695)

Juana de Asbaje was born in 1648 in the village of San Miguel de Nepantla, some forty-five miles from Mexico City, as the illegitimate daughter of a Spanish hidalgo and a Mexican woman (her use of her father's name indicates that at some point she was legitimized formally). Her parents moved almost immediately to the village of Amecameca, where the poet spent her childhood. At an early age the future poet showed extraordinary precocity: when she was six, having been taken to school with her elder sister in order to keep her out of her mother's way, she conceived an extraordinary passion for learning which was never thenceforth to leave her. In her *Respuesta a Sor Filotea*, she recounts that, having heard that eating cheese makes one dull of mind, she avoided that food scrupulously. At the age of ten or so she had already composed poems and plays and had also developed a consuming desire to study at the University of Mexico, proposing—presumably to the amusement of her family—that she assume male attire for this purpose.

The University was, of course, out of the question. Nevertheless, to Mexico City she went, her pleas having induced her mother to send her to the house of relatives residing there. She plunged enthusiastically into private study, concentrating especially on mathematics, science, philosophy, theology, and foreign languages (she had already mastered Latin and Greek before leaving Amecameca). At the age of sixteen she was presented at the court of the viceroy of Mexico, where both her learning and her extraordinary beauty endeared her to the vicereine, the Marquesa de Mancera. For three years she remained at court, as lady-in-waiting to the marquesa's daughter.

The pet of the court, Juana was also regarded as something of an oddity (was it worse or better that she was beautiful, one wonders). At one point, when she was in her early teens, she was interrogated by a group of learned men in a variety of disciplines, and she demonstrated a degree of knowledge that put them all to shame. One cannot help but be reminded of the New Testament account of the child Christ being similarly questioned: Juana, too, was to have her crucifixion. Concerning Juana's life at the viceregal court, there have been the inevitable speculations, none of them leading anywhere. It has been speculated that a Lesbian relationship developed between the vicereine and the brilliant adolescent; there is not a shred of evidence to support the speculation— which fact does not rule out the possibility. There has been speculation that Juana, during this time, experienced one or more passionate and unhappy affairs with one or more men. Again, no evidence—a fact which cannot refute the speculation. Certain it is that the poet Sor Juana Inés de la Cruz knew everything there is to know about sexual passion, and that she demonstrated this knowledge in her lyric poems. There are some who would say that her knowledge could only have been derived from personal experience. They may be wrong: Juana was one of the most intelligent people of her age (or, probably, of any age), and to the unusually intelligent many kinds of knowledge are possible. One cannot know. As usual, Juana eludes us, unlike Louise Labé and Gaspara Stampa, who are quite circumstantial about the bases of their passionate knowledge in actual experience.

In 1667, at the age of nineteen, Juana de Asbaje entered the covent of the Discalced Carmelites in Mexico City. She left as soon as she could, some three months later, presumably for reasons of health. In 1669 she entered the convent of the Hieronymite Order, where she was to remain until her death in 1695. The Carmelites are, of course, an order proverbial for their austerity; such is not the case with the Hieronymites, and, apparently, the young nun found in their midst a clean, well-lighted place—a reasonably comfortable cell equipped with scientific and musical instruments, with the best library in New Spain (her own), and with a steady stream of admiring and talkative visitors. Given the time and place in which she was unfortunate enough to be born, she could not have hoped for more.

Much ink has been squandered on the question of Sor Juana's religious vocation. It seems unnecessary to speculate, given what the poet herself tells us in her *Respuesta a Sor Filotea*:

> I became a religious because, although I knew that that estate entailed things very repugnant to my temperament (I speak of the incidentals, not of the essentials), it was, given the total aversion which I felt toward matrimony, the least unsuitable and the most honorable I could choose in respect to the security of my salvation which I wished. . . .[1]

In short, the convent was the lesser of the two evils that proposed themselves as the only alternatives for a respectable Mexican woman of the seventeenth century. For a poet living in a society that did not recognize the concept of the *grande dame,* that of the *femme savante,* or that of the *cortigiana onesta,* it was the only possible choice.

Sor Juana was not a mystic. The only basis one can imagine for that claim, one which is often made by students of her work, is the unexamined assumption that a literary nun *must* be a mystic. Sometimes, as in her *Romance* 56 ("En que expresa los efectos del Amor Divino, y propone morir amante, a pesar de todo riesgo"), she has mysticism as her subject, but, like John Donne in many of his *Divine Poems,* she expresses the *desire* for the beatific vision rather than the experience thereof. Neither the nonmystical nature of Sor Juana's temperament nor the nonreligious motivation for her taking the veil should be understood as implying any lack of religious belief. All the available evidence of her life and work suggests that she was a faithful Catholic Christian, firm in her faith and fully correct in her observance of its forms.

Her life as a nun was, indeed, subject to the incommodities for which she had been prepared—the friendly and loving but superdependent company of her fellow sisters, the partly welcome but partly intrusive visits of worldly people who wanted the brilliance of her conversation or the gift of a love poem appropriate to some particular situation. But there were compensations—above all, the opportunity to study, to learn, to think. Like Donne, Sor Juana was subject to "the worst voluptuousness, which is an hydroptic, immoderate desire of humane learning and languages";[2] in the convent she could, to some extent, satisfy that desire. More serious obstacles to her true vocation were certain ecclesiastical authorities and her own delicate health. At one point a narrow-minded prelate ordered her to cease her studies: she did as commanded, but, as she writes in the *Respuesta,* ". . . since it was not within my power to cease absolutely, I observed all things that God created, the universal machine serving me in place of books."[3] The prelate left office after a few months, but, Sor Juana having fallen ill, she was again forbidden to read, this time by her physicians. Seeing that the lack of books subjected her to still greater mental tension, they were obliged to withdraw the prohibition.[4]

In 1690 she was prevailed upon to write a critique of a somewhat unorthodox sermon published by a Portuguese Jesuit named Antonio Vieyra.[5] Without her knowledge or consent, her rebuttal was published under the title *Carta atenagórica;* it won her the admiration and praise of learned men not only in Spanish America but also in Spain and Portugal. It also elicited from her friend the bishop of Puebla in Mexico a letter composed under the pseudonym "Sor Filotea de la Cruz," a letter which, though praising Sor Juana for her learning and intelligence, reprimands her for having wasted so much time on worldly knowledge and profane letters and recommends that she devote her gifts entirely to theological study and the refutation of religious error.

It may all have been a put-up job. It is altogether possible that the bishop himself arranged for the publication of the *Carta atenagórica*, with the intention of using its success to force Juana into placing her genius exclusively at the service of the Church—for its greater glory and her more assured salvation. If this hypothesis is correct, the bishop was acting from motives that were far from mean or malicious. A man of the Church, he was doing his duty as he saw it by adding strength to the defense of the true faith and at the same time contributing to the spiritual welfare of a woman he sincerely admired. Nevertheless, however well-intentioned he may have been, he was responsible for the destruction of one of the finest literary artists of the Baroque, and the modern reader is likely to find it difficult to forgive him.

For Sor Juana took it hard. Her immediate response was an open letter, the great *Respuesta a Sor Filotea de la Cruz* (she knew perfectly well who lurked behind the pseudonym). One of the earliest documents of modern feminism, an exemplary piece of forceful argumentative prose, the *Respuesta* is also one of the noblest of all defenses of intellectual freedom. It is also the source of a good deal of what we know of Sor Juana's life. Juana maintains that her general lack of concentration on theological dispute or other kinds of specifically religious writing is to be traced not to any indifference on her part but to humility. She maintains, further, that most of her metrical compositions (she specifically excepts *El sueño*) were written as favors to importunate visitors and that they occupied little of her time or attention. But her principal point is woman's freedom to *learn*, in both sacred and secular fields, and she drives her argument home by pointing out that God Himself has placed in certain women the desire to learn and by citing a vast array of learned women throughout history, scriptural, classical, and contemporaneous. If the document is a defense of intellectual freedom, it is also a defense of reason (though always, be it noted, within the limits of Catholic orthodoxy), and some commentators have seen in it the influence of Descartes.[6]

Having unburdened her mind, Sor Juana Inés de la Cruz unburdened her life. She sold all her books, musical instruments, and scientific devices, giving the proceeds to the poor, and subjected herself to a course of rigorous penances. Inevitably, some authorities have posited an experience of spiritual awakening, possibly mystical in nature, as the basis of these actions.[7] It is more likely that, as Graves suggests,[8] she chose to deny her intellect rather than to falsify it by directing it exclusively to theology. At any rate, her confessor, Padre Antonio Nuñez de Miranda, though edified by her behavior, tried unsuccessfully to induce her to moderate it.

In 1695 the plague struck Mexico City. Having dedicated herself to nursing her stricken sisters, Juana caught the infection herself and died. She left behind a statement scrawled with her fingernail dipped in her own blood (she had forsworn the use of pen and ink):

> For the love of God and of His Purest Mother, I pray that my beloved sisters, both those now living and those who have gone before, will recommend me to Him—though I have been the worst woman in the world.[9]

A true Baroque artist, she ended in what one can only—perhaps a bit tearfully—classify as hyperbole.

What remains of this great soul and her intellectual passion? Several volumes of poems and plays, of surprising variety and uniform excellence. There are a number of dramatic works, including *autos sacramentales* and *loas* (different types of religious dramas) and *comedias* in the manner of Calderón; there are prose works, including the *Carta atenagórica* and the *Respuesta a Sor Filotea;* there are, finally, the lyric works, some of them occasional and complimentary, many of them amorous, many of them—including the ambitious and very difficult *Sueño*—philosophical. Sor Juana handles the general European lyric forms with great virtuosity; she is one of the most accomplished writers of sonnets that Western literature can boast. But she also, like most of the Peninsular poets of the *siglo de oro*, wrote in the indigenous Spanish forms—*romances, redondillas, silvas, liras*, etc.

Sor Juana's greatness as a lyric poet rests on a number of qualities— philosophical profundity and complexity, psychological astuteness (especially with regard to the relation of the sexes), and a superb mastery of the complex of techniques that in part makes up the Baroque style— ornate decoration, paradox and irony, wordplay, conceit, hyperbole, general extravagance of language, dramatic immediacy, and, most of all perhaps, what the seventeenth century called "wit" (Spanish *ingenio*)— which, implying a range of experience from simple playfulness to cosmic perception, might best be defined as the capacity for perceiving the resemblances among the apparently dissimilar. "Range" is an important term in characterizing Sor Juana's poetic work. As a philosophical poet she sometimes deploys the great commonplaces of poetic tradition (as in "Este que ves, engaño colorido" or "Rosa divina que en gentil cultura"); she sometimes contemplates the limitations and contradictions of human knowledge (as in "Acusa la hidropesía de mucha ciencia"); on at least one occasion *(El sueño)* she engages in original epistemological speculation. As a love poet she displays a range that extends from passionate avowals ("Esta tarde, mi bien, cuando te hablaba") to wryly hard-bitten observations on the ironies of sexual attraction ("Que no me quiere Fabio, al verse amado" and "Feliciano me adora y le aborrezco"). She has satirical power as well, best exemplified perhaps in the delightfully malicious *redondillas* "Hombres necios que acusais," the most biting expression of feminism produced by the seventeenth century.

Gaspara Stampa and Louise Labé are both magnificent poets, but Sor Juana Inés de la Cruz exceeds them in artistic stature. Her strongest affinities are with her somewhat older Spanish contemporary Francisco de Quevedo and, in England, with John Donne and Andrew Marvell. In other words, she is a Metaphysical poet, and she is one of the greatest.

NOTES

1. Quoted in G. Guernelli, *Gaspara Stampa, Louise Labé y Sor Juana Inés de la Cruz: Tríptico renacentista barroco* (San Juan, Universidad de Puerto Rico Press, 1972), p. 29. My translation.
2. Quoted in H. J. C. Grierson, ed., *The Poems of John Donne*, 2 vols. (Oxford, 1912), 2:5.
3. Quoted in R. Graves, *The Crowning Privilege* (London, 1955), p. 172.
4. Ibid.
5. Ludwig Pfandl, *Sor Juana Inés de la Cruz: La Décima Musa de Mexico*, trans. from the German by J. A. Ortega y Medina (Mexico City, 1963), pp. 95 ff., attributes her critique to the same "masculinity complex" that he feels explains her artistic activities. Pfandl's misunderstood and misapplied Freudianism is to be rejected.
6. Guernelli, *Gaspara Stampa*, p. 31.
7. See ibid. p. 31.
8. Graves, *Crowning Privilege*, p. 173.
9. Ibid.

Procura desmentir los elogios que a un retrato de la poetisa inscribió la verdad, que llama pasión

Este que ves, engaño colorido,
que del arte ostentando los primores,
con falsos silogismos de colores
es cauteloso engaño del sentido;

éste, en quien la lisonja ha pretendido
excusar de los años los horrores,
y venciendo del tiempo los rigores
triunfar de la vejez y del olvido,

es un vano artificio del cuidado,
es una flor al viento delicada,
es un resguardo inútil para el hado:
es una necia diligencia errada,
es un afán caduco y, bien mirado,
es cadáver, es polvo, es sombra, es nada.

Quéjase de la suerte: insinuá su aversión a los vicios, y justifica su divertimiento a las musas

En perseguirme, Mundo,¿qué interesas?
¿En qué te ofendo, cuando sólo intento
poner bellezas en mi entendimiento
y no mi entendimiento en las bellezas?

Yo no estimo tesoros ni riquezas;
y así, siempre me causa más contento
poner riquezas en mi pensamiento
que no mi pensamiento en las riquezas.

Y no estimo hermosura que, vencida,
es despojo civil de las edades,
ni riqueza me agrada fementida,
teniendo por mejor, en mis verdades,

88

She refutes the praises dedicated to her portrait

This that you see, a highly colored hoax
Which demonstrates the excellence of art,
Upon the senses plays its crafty jokes
With faulty syllogisms on its part.

This, with which flattery tries to evade
The unrelenting horrors of the years
And, conquering the sallies time has made,
To triumph over age and all its cares,

Is just a vain device of apprehension,
Is just a fragile flower in the wind,
Is just a vain defense against our lot,
Is a foolish and impossible intention,
Is labor lost, and, to the thoughtful mind,
Is but a corpse, is dust, is shade, is nought.

Complaining of fate, she affirms her aversion to vice and defends her dedication to the Muses

What so impels you, World, to find your duty
In persecuting me? Do I offend
In seeking to give beauty to my mind
Instead of giving all my mind to beauty?

I have no use for riches without measure;
It gives me far more comfort to collect
Treasure to donate to my intellect
Than to donate my intellect to pleasure.

I cannot deem it beauty which is fated
To be the spoil of time's remorseless strife,
Nor do faithless riches hold appeal for me;
For I hold it better, if the truth be stated,

consumir vanidades de la vida
que consumir la vida en vanidades.

———————————

En que da moral censura a una rosa, y en ella a sus semejantes

Rosa divina que en gentil cultura
eres, con tu fragante sutileza,
magisterio purpúreo en la belleza,
enseñanza nevada a la hermosura.

Amago de la humana arquitectura,
ejemplo de la vana gentileza,
en cuyo ser unió naturaleza
la cuna alegre y triste sepultura.

¡Cuán altiva en tu pompa, presumida,
soberbia, el riesgo de morir desdeñas,
y luego desmayada y encogida
de tu caduco ser das mustias señas,
con que con docta muerte y necia vida,
viviendo engañas y muriendo enseñas!

———————————

Escoge antes el morir que exponerse a los ultrajes de la vejez

Miró Celia una rosa que en el prado
ostentaba feliz la pompa vana
y con afeites de carmín y grana
bañaba alegre el rostro delicado;

y dijo:—Goza, sin temor del Hado,
el curso breve de tu edad lozana,
pues no podrá la muerte de mañana
quitarte lo que hubieres hoy gozado;

90

To waste away the vanity of life
Than to waste away my life in vanity.

She lectures a rose

Rose divine who, with your gentle breeding,
With the fragrant subtlety that you possess,
Are a crimson class in beauty worth our heeding,
A snowy seminar in loveliness;

Portentous image of the human frame,
Example of vain charm that none can save,
Where nature has united in one name
The joyous cradle and the somber grave:

In all your pomp how proudly you disdain,
Haughty one, the danger of your dying;
But later, faint and wrinkled, you impeach
With withered symbols your decrepit being;
From your learnèd death and foolish life we gain:
Living you deceive, dying you teach.

She would choose to die rather than expose herself to the outrages of old age

Celia gazed on a rose as in the field
It happily displayed its splendor vain
And with cosmetic carmine paint did gild
And bathe its fragile face so dyed in grain;

She said, "Enjoy your life's brief lovely course,
And do not fear the menaces of fate,
For the death that comes tomorrow cannot force
From you today the joys that grace your state.

y aunque llega la muerte presurosa
y tu fragante vida se te aleja,
no sientas el morir tan bella y moza:
mira que la experiencia te aconseja
que es fortuna morirte siendo hermosa
y no ver el ultraje de ser vieja.

"Verde embeleso de la vida humana"

Verde embeleso de la vida humana,
loca Esperanza, frenesí dorado,
sueño de los despiertos intrincado
como de sueños, de tesoros vana;

alma del mundo, senectud lozana,
decrépito verdor imaginado;
el hoy de los dichosos esperado
y de los desdichados el mañana:

sigan tu sombra en busca de tu día
los que, con verdes vidrios por anteojos,
todo lo ven pintado a su deseo;
que yo más cuerdo en la fortuna mía,
tengo en entrambas manos ambos ojos
y solamente lo que toco veo.

En que satisface un recelo con la retórica del llanto

Esta tarde, mi bien, cuando te hablaba,
como en tu rostro y tus acciones vía
que con palabras no te persuadiá,
que el corazón me vieses deseaba;

And although death so swiftly will arrive,
And your fragrant life so quickly flee from you,
So fair and young you shall not feel death's hold:
Take counsel while your life and beauty thrive:
Fortune it is to die while gifts become you,
And not to see the outrage of being old."

"Green fascination of our human life"

Green fascination of our human life,
Mad Hope, thou frenzy gilded all with gold,
Dream of the waking, in which we behold
A tissue of dreams with empty treasures rife;

Soul of the world, senility in flower,
Decrepit greenness which our fancies feign,
The desired today the fortune attain,
And for the desperate tomorrow's hour:

Let them thy shade pursue in hope to find
Thy promised day, who green eyeglasses wear,
And see the world with their desire painted;
Let me, more prudent, seek in different kind;
In both my hands my two eyes let me bear,
Only with what I touch my sight acquainted.

The rhetoric of tears

Tonight, my dearest, when I spoke to thee,
I noted in thy bearing and thy face
That words of mine could not thy doubts erase,
Or prove I wanted thee my heart to see;

y Amor, que mis intentos ayudaba,
venció lo que imposible parecía:
pues entre el llanto, que el dolor vertía,
el corazón deshecho destilaba.

Baste ya de rigores, mi bien, baste;
no te atormenten más celos tiranos,
ni el vil recelo tu quietud contraste
con sombras necias, con indicios vanos,
pues ya en líquido humor viste y tocaste
mi corazón deshecho entre tus manos.

———————

Que contiene una fantasía contenta con amor decente

Detente, sombra di mi bien esquivo,
imagen del hechizo que más quiero,
bella ilusión por quien alegre muero,
dulce ficción por quien penosa vivo.

Si al imán de tus gracias, attractivo,
sirve mi pecho de obediente acero.
¿para qué me enamoras lisonjero
si has de burlarme luego fugitivo?

Mas blasonar no puedes, satisfecho,
de que triunfa de mí tu tiranía:
que aunque dejas burlado el lazo estrecho
que tu forma fantástica ceñía,
poco importa burlar brazos y pecho
si te labra prisión mi fantasía.

———————

Then love, which my avowals came to prop,
Conquered, and the impossible occurred:
I fell to weeping tears which sorrow poured,
Which my melting heart distilled in copious drop.

No more reproaches, ah my love, forbear;
Let doubt not hold thee in tormenting bonds,
Nor let vile jealousy thy peace impair
With foolish shades, with vain and useless wounds,
Since thou hast seen and touched a liquid rare—
My molten heart caught up between thy hands.

In which she restrains a fantasy, satisfying it with decent love

Stay, elusive shadow that I cherish,
Image of the enchantment which I love,
Illusion fair for which I gladly perish,
Sweet fiction for whose sake in pain I live.

If my breast responds to your attractive graces
As to the magnet the obedient steel,
Why woo me with your flattering embraces,
To flee me later, mocking my appeal?

But you cannot in satisfaction boast
That your tyranny has triumphed over me:
Even if you escape the noose I fashioned
To bind the form of your evasive ghost,
It matters not to flee my arms impassioned,
If you're imprisoned in my fantasy.

Resuelve la cuestión de cuál sea pesar más molesto en encontradas correspondencias, amar o aborrecer

Que no me quiera Fabio, al verse amado,
es dolor sin igual en mí sentido;
mas que me quiera Silvio, aborrecido,
es menor mal, mas no menos enfado.

¿Qué sufrimiento no estará cansado
si siempre le resuenan al oído
tras las vana arrogancia de un querido
el cansado gemir de un desdeñado?

Si de Silvio me cansa el rendimiento,
a Fabio canso con estar rendida;
si de éste busco el agradecimiento,
a mí me busca el otro agradecida:
por activa y pasiva es mi tormento,
pues padezco en querer y en ser querida.

――――――――――

Continúa el mismo asunto y aun le expresa con más viva elegancia

Feliciano me adora y le aborrezco;
Lisardo me aborrece y yo le adoro;
por quien no me apetece ingrato, lloro,
y al que me llora tierno, no apetezco.

A quien más me desdora, el alma ofrezco;
a quien me ofrece víctimas, desdoro;
desprecio al que enriquece mi decoro,
y al que le hace desprecios, enriquezco.

Si con mi ofensa al uno reconvengo,
me reconviene el otro a mí, ofendido;
y a padecer de todos modos vengo,
    pues ambos atormentan mi sentido:

She resolves the question of which is harder to bear, loving or hating

> That Fabio, whom I love, declines to love me
> Is a grief that has no equal in my brain;
> That Silvio, whom I can't bear, still wants to have me
> Is not as bad, but still gives me a pain.
>
> Whose patience would not be at length worn out
> At having always either one orating:
> The one she loves, the vain and haughty lout,
> Or the moaning, groaning one she can't help hating?
>
> If I'm bored to tears by Silvio's devotion,
> I'm bored to death adoring Fabio;
> If I seek to wake the latter man's emotion,
> The former man would have my feelings moved:
> The active and the passive plague me so;
> I hurt both in loving and in being loved.

On the same subject . . . but with more elegance

> Feliciano loves me and I abhor him;
> I love Lisardo, but he can't abide me;
> The indifferent ingrate makes me weep inside me,
> And the one who weeps for me . . . I can't endure him.
>
> To the one who slanders me my soul I offer,
> While I slander him who trophies to me raises;
> I scorn the one who freely sings my praises;
> To the one who scorns me . . . all I have I proffer.
>
> If I reproach the one, being offended,
> The other one, offended, hurls reproaches;
> And there's no way my sorrows can be mended,
> Since both torment with different approaches:

aquéste, con pedir lo que no tengo;
y aquél, con no tener lo que le pido.

Que da medio para amor sin mucha pena

Yo no puedo tenerte ni dejarte,
ni sé por qué, al dejarte o al tenerte,
se encuentra un no sé qué para quererte
y muchos sí sé qué para olvidarte.

Pues ni quieres dejarme ni enmendarte,
yo templaré mi corazón de suerte
que la mitad se incline a aborrecerte
aunque la otra mitad se incline a amarte.

Si ello es fuerza querernos, haya modo,
que es morir el estar siempre riñendo:
no se hable más en celo y en sospecha,
y quien da la mitad, no quiera el todo;
y cuando me las estás allá haciendo,
sabe que estoy haciendo la deshecha.

Acusa la hidropesía de mucha ciencia, que teme inútil aun para saber y nociva para vivir

Finjamos que soy feliz,
triste Pensamiento, un rato;
quizá podréis persuadirme,
aunque yo sé lo contrario:

que pues sólo en la aprehensión
dicen que estriban los daños,

What I haven't got one man's always commanding;
And the other hasn't got what I'm demanding.

A method of loving

I cannot either keep you or reject you,
Nor know I why, should I depart or stay,
I-know-not-what my heart to love doth sway,
Though I-do-know-what doth urge me to forget you.

Since you will neither leave me nor amend,
I shall reform my heart in such a fashion
That half of it shall hate you with a passion
And half of it shall still to love you bend.

Let's find a way, if love must us control;
in constant quarreling we both do die:
Let's speak no more in jealousy or doubt.
Who give but half should not desire the whole;
And when you do, deceiving, elsewhere lie,
Be sure that what I do you'll ne'er find out.

She condemns the hydropsy of excessive knowledge

Let us pretend, for a little bit,
That I am happy, sad Reflection;
Although I know the opposite,
Perhaps you can change my thought's direction:

For they say that all the harms we know
Come to us from our apprehension;

si os imagináis dichoso
no seréis tan desdichado.

Sírvame él entendimiento
alguna vez de descanso,
y no siempre esté el ingenio
con el provecho encontrado.

Todo el mundo es opiniones
de pareceres tan varios,
que lo que el uno que es negro,
el otro prueba que es blanco.

A unos sirve de atractivo
lo que otro concibe enfado;
y lo que éste por alivio,
aquél tiene por trabajo.

El que está triste, censura
al alegre de liviano;
y el que está alegre, se burla
de ver al triste penando.

Los dos Filósofos Griegos
bien esta verdad probaron:
pues lo que en el uno risa,
causaba en el otro llanto.

Célebre su oposición
ha sido por siglos tantos,
sin que cuál acertó, esté
hasta agora averiguado;

antes, en sus dos banderas
el mundo todo alistado,
conforme el humor le dicta,
sigue cada cual el bando.

Uno dice que de risa
sólo es digno el mundo vario;

If you pretend you're happy, though,
Your sorrow won't claim such attention.

Let my intelligence sustain
For once, and serve to comfort me;
Let not my ever-searching brain
Oppose my own felicity.

The world's appearances deceive;
Opinions clash like day and night:
One man will something black perceive,
Another man will prove it white.

Some feel a powerful attraction
To what repels another one;
And what one person finds distraction
Another views as work to be done.

The sober man extends his censure
To the jolly one, as light of mind;
While the jolly one a laugh will venture
To see the sad one sorrows find.

The two philosophers of Greece[1]
Provide convincing demonstration:
What caused in one a laugh's release
Provoked in the other lamentation.

Famous has been their opposition
Throughout so many centuries,
But neither philosopher's position
Has proved itself: no one agrees.

Quite otherwise, under two banners
The entire world itself enlists;
According to one's mood and manners
One chooses sides and then persists.

One says that all this world so various
Is worthy but of laughs and jeers;

1. Democritus and Heraclitus.

y otro, que sus infortunios
son sólo para llorados.

Para todo se halla prueba
y razón en que fundarlo;
y no hay razón para nada,
de haber razón para tanto.

Todos son iguales jueces;
y siendo iguales y varios
no hay quien pueda decidir
cuál es lo más acertado.

Pues, si no hay quien lo sentencie,
¿por qué pensáis, vos, errado,
que os cometió Dios a vos
la decisión de los casos?

¿O por qué, contra vos mismo
severamente inhumano,
entre lo amargo y lo dulce,
quereis elegir lo amargo?

Si es mío mi entendimiento
¿por qué siempre he de encontrarlo
tan torpe para el alivio,
tan agudo para el daño?

El discurso es un acero
que sirve por ambos cabos;
de dar muerte, por la punta;
por el pomo, de resguardo.

Si vos, sabiendo el peligro,
queréis por la punta usarlo,
¿qué culpa tiene el acero
del mal uso de la mano?

No es saber, saber hacer
discursos sutiles, vanos;
que el saber consiste sólo
en elegir lo más sano.

Another that its griefs nefarious
Give just occasion for our tears.

For everything a proof you'll find
And reason upon which it's founded;
Reason to nothing is assigned,
If on reason so many things are grounded.

As judges, all men count as peers,
Each one a different view affirming;
And no one qualified appears
To say who's right: there's no confirming.

Then, if there is no judge appointed
To settle matters, why assume
That you have been by God anointed
To pass on every question's doom?

Or why, against yourself severe,
To the point of being inhumane,
When bitter and sweet together appear,
Must you the bitter choice maintain?

If my intellect to me belongs,
Why do I find it so perverse:
So sluggish to relieve my wrongs,
So keen to make my troubles worse?

Reason is a sharpened steel;
Both ends are useful in a strife:
The point is ready death to deal;
The pommel guards its owner's life.

If you, of danger still aware,
Insist on holding it by the blade,
What guilt does the hapless sword incur
For the awkwardness the hand's displayed?

To know is not to formulate
A vain and subtle disquisition;
To know is to ameliorate,
By choosing wisely, one's condition.

103

Especular las desdichas
y examinar los presagios,
sólo sirve de que el mal
crezca con anticiparlo.

En los trabajos futuros,
la atención, sutilizando,
más formidable que el riesgo
suele fingir lo amargo.

¡Qué feliz es la ignorancia
del que, indoctamente sabio,
halla de lo que padece,
en lo que ignora, sagrado!

No siempre suben seguros
vuelos del ingenio osados,
que buscan trono en el fuego
y hallan sepulcro en el llanto.

También es vicio el saber:
que si no se va atajando,
cuando menos se conoce
es más nocivo el estrago;

y si el vuelo no le abaten,
en sutilezas cebado,
por cuidar de lo curioso
olvida lo necesario.

Si culta mano no impide
crecer al àrbol copado,
quita la substancia al fruto
la locura de los ramos.

Si andar a nave ligera
no estorba lastre pesado,
sirve el vuelo de que sea
el precipicio más alto.

En amenidad inútil,
¿qué importa al florido campo,

To speculate on one's misfortune,
And signs and presages to scan,
Serves only evil to importune
And sorrow by design to plan.

Subtly to direct attention
To the heavy trials the future brings
Is to give a perilous extension
To the threat that lies in common things.

How blessed is the ignorance
Of him, in lack of learning wise,
To whom not knowing kindly grants
Refuge from what his lot implies!

The flights attempted by the mind
Don't always find a safe ascent,
For they seek a throne in fire but find
A sepulchre in sad lament.

Knowledge is a vice as well:
If you don't give it firm instruction,
It will, just when you least can tell,
Inflict a terrible destruction.

And if you don't restrain its flight,
It will, fed full with niceties,
On curiosities alight,
Ignoring the necessities.

If a well-trained hand neglects to prune
The growth of the overweening tree,
The substance of the fruit will soon
To the madly growing branches flee.

If on a ship that is too light
A heavy ballast is not laid,
The very swiftness of its flight
Will to a sharper ruin lead.

What profit to the flowering field,
In useless beauty bright and gay,

si no halla fruto el Otoño,
que ostente flores el Mayo?

¿De qué le sirve al ingenio
el producir muchos partos,
si a la multitud se sigue
el malogro de abortarlos?

Y a esta desdicha por fuerza
ha de seguirse el fracaso
de quedar el que produce,
si no muerto, lastimado.

El ingenio es como el fuego:
que, con la materia ingrato,
tanto la consume más
cuanto él se ostenta más claro.

Es de su propio Señor
tan rebelado vasallo,
que convierte en sus ofensas
las armas de su resguardo.

Este pésimo ejercicio,
este duro afán pesado,
a los hijos de los hombres
dio Dios para ejercitarlos.

¿Qué loca ambición nos lleva
de nosotros olvidados?
Si es para vivir tan poco,
¿de qué sirve saber tanto?

¿Oh, si como hay de saber,
hubiera algún seminario
o escuela donde a ignorar
se enseñaran los trabajos!

¡Qué felizmente viviera
el que, flojamente cauto,
burlara las amenazas
del influjo de los astros!

If in Autumn it no fruit will yield,
To be showing off its flowers in May?

What profit to the intellect
To be so fertile in conception,
If the numerous progeny are wrecked,
Aborted quite from their inception?

And it follows of necessity
That she whom this misfortune hounded
Remains, after calamity,
If not quite dead, most badly wounded.

The intellect is like a fire:
Implacably opposed to matter,
The more it eats it up entire,
It shows itself just that much brighter.

It proves a vassal in such revolt
Against its due and proper lord
That it turns to an offensive bolt
The arms that should defense afford.

God gave unto the sons of men
This worst of all activities,
This harsh and heavy weight, that then
It might train their proclivities.

What mad ambition transports us so,
Forgetful of our proper weal?
If our days of life so swiftly go,
Why has knowledge such appeal?

If only there were a seminary,
Where, instead of learning how to learn,
One could bend one's efforts to be wary
Of knowledge, and could ignorance earn!

How happily might one then live,
Negligently being careful,
Making fun of the stars above,
Whose influence seems to be so fearful!

Aprendamos a ignorar,
Pensamiento, pues hallamos
que cuanto añado al discurso,
tanto le usurpo a los años.

Arguye de inconsecuentes el gusto y la censura de los hombres que en las mujeres acusan lo que causan

Hombres necios que acusáis
a la mujer sin razón,
sin ver que sois la ocasión
de lo mismo que culpáis:

si con ansia sin igual
solicitáis su desdén,
¿por qué queréis que obren bien
si las incitáis al mal?

Combatis su resistencia
y luego, con gravedad,
decís que fue liviandad
lo que hizo la diligencia.

Parecer quiere el denuedo
de vuestro parecer loco,
al niño que pone el coco
y luego le tiene miedo.

Queréis, con presunción necia,
hallar a la que buscáis,
para pretendida, Thais,
y en la posesión, Lucrecia.

¿Qué humor puede ser más raro
que el que, falto de consejo,
él mismo empaña el espejo,
y siente que no esté claro?

Con el favor y el desdén
tenéis condición igual,

Let's strive then ignorance to gain,
My Intellect, since it appears
That whatever is added to the brain
Is promptly subtracted from one's years.

———————————

**In which she condemns the inconsistency of men, who blame women
for what they themselves have caused**

Stupid men, fond of abusing
All women, without any shame,
Not seeing you're the ones to blame
For the very faults that you're accusing:

If, with a single-minded will,
You seek her well-deserved disdain,
Why do you want her to remain
Good, while inciting her to ill?

You strive to conquer her resistance,
Then with a solemn treachery
Attribute to her lechery
What was only done through your persistence.

Your mad position seems to fit
That of a child who draws a spook
And, when he dares to take a look,
Finds that he's afraid of it.

Showing presumptuous indiscretion,
You want to find her you're pursuing
To be Thais while you are wooing
And Lucretia when she's in possession.

What quirky humor could be more queer
Than his who, from all reason banned,
Smudges a mirror with his hand,
Then whines because it isn't clear?

If favor or disdain we tell,
You give us the same reception, madly—

quejándoos, si os tratan mal,
burlándoos, si os quieren bien.

Opinión, ninguna gana;
pues la que más se recata,
si no os admite, es ingrata,
y si os admite, es liviana.

Siempre tan necios andáis
que, con desigual nivel,
a una culpáis por cruël
y a otra por fácil culpáis.

¿Pues cómo ha de estar templada
la que vuestro amor pretende,
si la que es ingrata, ofende,
y la que es fácil, enfada?

Mas, entre el enfado y pena
que vuestro gusto refiere,
bien haya la que no os quiere
y quejáos en hora buena.

Dan vuestras amantes penas
a sus libertades alas,
y después de hacerlas malas
las queréis hallar muy buenas.

¿Cuál mayor culpa ha tenido
en una pasión, errada:
la que cae de rogada,
o el que ruega de caído?

¿O cuál es más de culpar,
aunque cualquiera mal haga:
la que peca por la paga,
o el que paga por pecar?

Pues ¿para qué os espantáis
de la culpa que tenéis?
Queredlas cual las hacéis
o hacedlas cual las buscáis.

Complaining when we treat you badly,
And sneering when we treat you well.

No female reputation's sure:
The most cautious woman in the town
Is an ingrate if she turns you down;
If she gives in to you she's a whore.

In stupidity you're all the same,
Each one an inconsistent fool;
You blame one girl for being cruel,
While the yielding one you also blame.

Your expectation is truly curious,
Of the woman who would seek your love;
The one who's ungrateful you reprove,
And the one who's available makes you furious.

But whatever the rage, whatever the plaints
That your capricious minds may fashion,
Lucky is one who feels no passion;
Just go somewhere else with your complaints.

Your amorous blandishments give wing
To a lady's libertine inclination,
But having seduced her in sinful fashion,
You want her to be a most virtuous thing.

In the errant passion two may loll in,
Whose fault would you describe as baser:
Hers who falls because you chase her,
Or his who chases because he's fallen?

Or who the greater guilt does win,
Whatever shameful pact is made:
She who sins because she's paid,
Or he who pays so he may sin?

But why do you pretend to be
Surprised at your sins, when you've displayed them?
Wish women to be what you have made them,
Or make them what you'd like to see.

Dejad de solicitar,
y después, con más razón,
acusaréis, la afición
de la que os fuere a rogar.

Bien con muchas armas fundo
que lidia vuestra arrogancia,
pues en promesa e instancia
juntáis diablo, carne y mundo.

Que expresan sentimientos de ausente

Amado dueño mío,
escucha un rato mis cansadas quejas,
pues del viento las fío,
que breve las conduzca a tus orejas,
si no se desvanece el triste acento
como mis esperanzas en el viento.

Óyeme con los ojos,
ya que están tan distantes los oídos,
y de ausentes enojos
en ecos, de mi pluma mis gemidos;
y ya que ti no llega mi voz ruda,
óyeme sordo, pues me quejo muda.

Si del campo te agradas,
goza de sus frescuras venturosas,
sin que aquestas cansadas
lágrimas te detengan, enfadosas;
que en él verás, si atento te entretienes,
ejemplos de mis males y mis bienes.

Si al arroyo parlero
ves, galán de las flores en el prado,
que, amante y lisonjero,
a cuantas mira intima su cuidado,
en su corriente mi dolor te avisa
que a costa de mi llanto tiene risa.

Stop your own solicitations,
And then you may possess the right
To accuse a girl of being light
When she comes to you with unchaste persuasions.

Your arrogance fights on every level,
I note, with strong and well-aimed batteries,
For with ceaseless promises and flatteries
You unite the world, the flesh, the devil.

She expresses the feeling of an absent lover

My dear belovèd lord,
Give ear a moment to my sad laments,
As the wind bears them abroad
To take them swiftly to your ears from hence,
Unless the sorrowing tones that I do send
Are, like my hopes, dispersèd by the wind.

Hear me with your eyes,
Since your ears remain so distant from my ken;
Hear my distant sighs
Whose sobbing echoes issue through my pen;
And since my rough voice cannot you attain,
Hear me deafly, while mutely I complain.

If by the field you're pleasured,
Enjoy the happy freshness of its being;
Let not these tears unmeasured
Disturb you in enjoying it, for, seeing,
You'll note, if you're attentive to its shows,
Examples of my blisses and my woes.

If the babbling stream you see,
True lover of the field and of the flowers,
Spend amorous flattery,
To all it views imparting its sad cares,
In its current you may recognize my sorrow,
And at my tears' expense may laughter borrow.

113

Si ves que triste llora
su esperanza marchita, en ramo verde,
tórtola gemidora,
en él y en ella mi dolor te acuerde,
que imitan, con verdor y con lamento,
él mi esperanza y ella mi tormento.

Si la flor delicada,
si la peña, que altiva no consiente
del tiempo ser hollada,
ambas me imitan, aunque variamente,
ya con fragilidad, ya con dureza,
mi dicha aquella y ésta mi firmeza.

Si ves el ciervo herido
que baja por el monte, acelerado,
buscando, dolorido,
alivio al mal en un arroyo helado,
y sediento al cristal se precipita,
no en el alivio, en el dolor me imita.

Si la liebre encogida
huye medrosa de los galgos fieros,
y por salvar la vida
no deja estampa de los pies ligeros,
tal mi esperanza, en dudas y recelos,
se ve acosada de villanos celos.

Si ves el cielo claro,
tal es la sencillez del alma mía;
y si, de luz avaro,
de tinieblas se emboza el claro día,
es con su obscuridad y su inclemencia,
imagen de mi vida en esta ausencia.

Así que, Fabio amado,
saber puedes mis males sin costarte
la noticia cuidado,
pues puedes de los campos informarte;
y pues yo a todo mi dolor ajusto,
saber mi pena sin dejar tu gusto.

Mas ¿cuándo, ¡ay gloria mía!,
mereceré gozar tu luz serena?

If you see the turtle-dove
On a green branch his withered hope bewailing,
In groans that still must move,
May branch and dove my sorrow unavailing
Recall to you: green branch and sad lament
At once my hope and torment represent.

If you see the fragile flower,
Or the crag that proudly scorns to be the prey
Of time's relentless hour,
Observe the different ways they me portray
In frailness one denotes my happiness;
In hardness the other my firmness does express.

If you see the wounded stag
Who hastens, suffering, longing for relief,
Down the mountainside,
In search of some icy brook to soothe his grief,
And thirsting into the crystal dives amain,
He imitates me, not in relief, in pain.

If the timid rabbit flees
In terror from the savage hounds pursuing,
And to save his life betrays
No print of where his agile feet are going,
Just so my hopes perceive themselves to be
Traced down by doubts and ugly jealousy.

If you see the brilliant sky,
Even such is my simplicity of soul;
And if the cloudy day,
Miser of light, is wrapped in shady pall,
In its darkness and its rigor you may read
The image of the lonely life I lead.

Thus, Fabio, my love
You may learn without distress about my pains,
And they need not remove
Your pleasures, since these fields will give you signs;
Since to everything therein I match my sorrow,
You can know my grief but need not let it harrow.

But when, my glory, say
Will I deserve to taste your light serene?

115

¿Cuándo llegará el día
que pongas dulce fin a tanta pena?
¿Cuándo veré tus ojos, dulce encanto,
y de los míos quitarás el llanto?

¿Cuándo tu voz sonora
herirá mis oídos, delicada,
y el alma que te adora,
de inundación de gozos anegada,
a recibirte con amante prisa
saldrá a los ojos desatada en risa?

¿Cuándo tu luz hermosa
revestirá de gloria mis sentidos?
¿Y cuándo yo, dichosa,
mis suspiros daré por bien perdidos,
teniendo en poco el precio de mi llanto,
que tanto ha de penar quien goza tanto?

¿Cuándo de tu apacible
rostro alegre veré el semblante afable,
y aquel bien indecible
a toda humana pluma inexplicable,
que mal se ceñirá a lo definido
lo que no cabe en todo lo sentido?

Ven pues, mi prenda amada:
que ya fallece mi cansada vida
de esta ausencia pesada;
ven, pues: que mientras tarda tu venida,
aunque me cueste su verdor enojos,
regaré mi esperanza con mis ojos.

Sueño (selección)

Piramidal, funesta, de la tierra
nacida sombra, al Cielo encaminaba
de vanos obeliscos punta altiva,

116

And when will dawn the day
That will make a sweet conclusion to my pain?
When, sweet enchanter, will your eyes appear,
And when, from mine, will you remove the tear?

When will your sounding voice
Strike my ears with a delicious pain,
And when will, drowned in joys,
The soul that loves you find its bliss again,
And in loving haste, the sight of you to capture,
Will it fill my eyes dissolved in laughing rapture?

When will your light so fair
Clothe in glory all my startled senses?
And when shall I declare
That all the sighs I've spent are fair expenses,
Holding at little price my tears, for such
One has to pay if one will joy so much?

When shall I see again
The pleasing features of your happy face,
And feel the joy no pen
Is capable of uttering with grace?
For poorly would the definite contain
That which exceeds the compass of the brain.

Come then, belovèd treasure:
My weary life already starts to fade
In this absence without measure;
Come then, for while your arrival is delayed,
Although its greenness costs me many sighs,
My hope I'll go on watering with my eyes.

––––––––––

The dream (selection)

Pyramidal, funereal, earth-born,
A shadow toward the sky itself directed,
With the proud point of its vain obelisk

escalar pretendiendo las Estrellas;
si bien sus luces bellas
—exentas siempre, siempre rutilantes—
la tenebrosa guerra
que con negros vapores le intimaba
la pavorosa sombra fugitiva
burlaban tan distantes,
que su atezado ceño
al superior convexo aun no llegaba
del orbe de la Diosa
que tres veces hermosa
con tres hermosos rostros ser ostenta,
quedando sólo dueño
del aire que empañaba
con el aliento denso que exhalaba;
y en la quietud contenta
de imperio silencioso,
sumisas sólo voces consentía
de las nocturnas aves,
tan obscuras, tan graves,
que aun el silencio no se interrumpía.

Con tardo vuelo y canto, del oído
mal, y aun peor del ánimo admitido,
la avergonzada Nictimene acecha
de las sagradas puertas los resquicios,
o de las claraboyas eminentes
los huecos más propicios
que capaz a su intento le abren brecha,
y sacrílega llega a los lucientes
faroles sacros de perenne llama
que extingue, si no infama,
en licor claro la materia crasa
consumiendo, que el árbol de Minerva
de su fruto, de prensas agravado,
congojoso sudó y rindió forzado.

Y aquellas que su casa
campo vieron volver, sus telas hierba,
a la deidad de Baco inobedientes
—ya no historias contando diferentes,
en forma sí afrentosa transformadas—
segunda forman niebla,

Aspiring to climb up to the stars;
But their light so beautiful
—Always clear and always sparkling—
Did mock the twilit war
By the fearsome fleeting shadow just declared,
So that its blackened frown
Did not reach to the convex upper surface
Of the sphere-enthronèd Goddess
Who shows herself thrice lovely
With the three lovely faces she displays;
And thus was left the master
Of nothing but the air,
Which it tarnished with the dense breath it exhaled;
And, contented with the quiet
Of its ever-silent empire,
Permitted only the soft submissive voices
Of the feathered race nocturnal,
So dark, so grave, so heavy,
That scarcely was the silence interrupted.

   With sluggish flight and song, scarcely accepted
By the ear, even less accepted by the soul,
Shameful Nyctimene[1] does lurk as spy
At the chinks of sacred doors or at the hollows
Propitious of the skylights,
Opening sufficient breach to suit her,
And, sacrilegious, the sacred, gleaming lamps
Of perpetual flame she reaches and puts out,
If not even defiles,
Consuming the fat substance of the liquor
So clear, which that tree sacred to Minerva[2]
In anguish sweated and yielded of its fruit
Under force borne down beneath the weight of presses.

   And those maidens who beheld
Their house transformed to field, to grass their garments,
They being to god Bacchus disobedient
—No longer telling differing accounts,
Turned now to shapes so ignominious—
They form a second mist,

---

1. The owl. / 2. The olive.

ser vistas aun temiendo en la tiniebla,
aves sin pluma aladas:
aquellas tres oficíosas, digo,
atrevidas Hermanas,
que el tremendo castigo
de desnudas les dió pardas membranas
alas tan mal dispuestas
que escarnio son aun de las más funestas:
éstas, con el parlero
ministro de Plutón un tiempo, ahora
supersticioso indicio al agorero,
solos la no canora
componían capilla pavorosa,
máximas, negras, longas entonando,
y pausas más que voces, esperando
a la torpe mensura perezosa
de mayor proporción tal vez, que el viento
con flemático echaba movimiento,
de tan tardo compás, tan detenido,
queen medio se quedó tal vez dormido.

Este, pues, triste són intercadente
de la asombrada turba temerosa,
menos a la atención solicitaba
que al sueño persuadía;
antes sí, lentamente,
su obtusa consonancia espacíosa
al sosiego inducía
y al reposo los miembros convidaba
—el silencio intimando a los vivientes,
uno y otro sellando labio obscuro
con indicante dedo,
Harpócrates, la noche, silencioso;
a cuyo, aunque no duro,
si bien imperioso
precepto, todos fueron obedientes—

El viento sosegado, el can dormido,
éste yace, aquél quedo
los átomos no mueve,
con el susurro hacer temiendo leve,
aunque poco; sacrílego ruído,
violador del silencio sosegado.
El mar, no ya alterado,

Still fearing to be seen amid night's shades,
Birds wingèd but unplumed:
I mean those three officious daring sisters,[3]
Whom the punishment tremendous
Gave for wings dark-webbèd naked membranes,
So ill-arranged that they
Derision rouse amid the most ghastly birds:
They, together with
The minister of Pluto, once loquacious,[4]
Now an ill omen grown for the fortune-teller,
Made up among themselves
The frightful choir so unmelodious,
Their minims, crotchets, quavers still intoning,
And in pauses more than tones sometimes awaiting
The heavy lazy measure which the wind,
In proportion far grander chose to mark
With movement so phlegmatic and prolonged
That in between it sometimes fell asleep.

Thus, then, interposing a sad sound
Amid the timorous astonished throng,
It less demanded of itself attention
Than it to sleep induced;
On the contrary, quite slowly,
A thick and spacious harmony imposed
Calm quiet peace,
And Harpocrates, the night, did every member
Invite, with warning finger, to repose
—Announcing silence to all living things,
And each and every lip with darkness sealing;
And to this precept clear,
Not hard, although imperious,
All things at large at once became obedient.

The pacified wind, the sleeping dog—the latter
Lies still; the former, silent
Does not disturb the atoms,
Fearing lest the slightest rustle make
Though slight, disturbing sacrilegious sound,
Of slumbrous silence senseless violator.
The sea, not yet transformed,

---

3. The three daughters of Minyas. / 4. Ascalaphus, the loquacious servant of Hades.

ni aun la instable mecía
cerúlea cuna donde el Sol dormía;
y los dormidos, siempre mudos, peces,
en los lechos lamosos
de sus obscuros senos cavernosos,
mudos eran dos veces;
Y entre ellos, la engañosa encantadora
Alcione, a los que antes
en peces transformó, simples amantes,
transformada también, vengaba ahora.

En los del monte senos escondidos,
cóncavos de pañascos mal formados
—de su aspereza menos defendidos
que de su obscuridad asegurados—
cuya mansión sombría
ser puede noche en la mitad del dia,
incógnita aún al cierto
montaraz pie del cazador experto
—depuesta la fiereza
de unos, y de otros el temor depuesto—
yacía el vulgo bruto,
a la Naturaleza
el de su potestad pagando impuesto,
universal tributo;
y el Rey, que vigilancias afectaba,
aun con abiertos ojos no velaba.

El de sus mismos perros acosado,
monarca en otro tiempo esclarecido,
tímido ya venado,
con vigilante oído,
del sosegado ambiente
al menor perceptible movimiento
que los átomos muda,
la oreja alterna aguda
y el leve rumor siente
que aun lo altera dormido.
Y en la quietud del nido,
que de brozas y lodo instable hamaca
formó en la más opaca
parte del árbol, duerme recogida
la leve turba, descansando el viento
del que le corta, alado movimiento.

Rocked not the unstable cradle,
Cerulean refuge where the sun was sleeping;
And the sleeping, ever-silent fish,
Within the slimy beds
Of their dark and cavernous recesséd lairs,
Were couchéd doubly mute;
And among them the enchantress so deceitful,
Halcyon, who now took vengeance,
Herself transformed, upon the simple lovers
Whom she before had metamorphosed to fishes.

Within the caverns by the mountain hidden,
Hollows ill-formed by grim and rocky crags
—Less, one might say, by their ruggedness defended
Than by their safe obscurity assured—
Whose dwelling shady night
Appears, even in the middle of the day,
Unknown even to the foot
Assured and savage of the skillful hunter
—Setting aside the fierceness
Of some, and of others the fear setting aside—
Here couched the mob of beasts,
To Nature tribute paying,
The universal impost due its power;
And the King,[5] who every diligence asserted,
Even with open eyes did not keep watch.

He who by his own dogs was hunted down,[6]
In other times a much-renownéd monarch,
And now a timid stag,
Of the hushed atmosphere
Each slightest movement that might be perceived
Which alters any atoms
He notes with sharpened ear
And hears the lightest rustle
Which disturbs him even in the depths of sleep.
And in the quiet nest,
Unstable hammock formed of mud and brushwood
In the most opaque recesses
Of the tree, there sleeps tight-huddled
The feathered throng; and now the wind is resting
From the wingéd movements that were wont to cut it.

---

5. The lion. / 6. Actaeon.

De Júpiter el ave generosa
—como al fin Reina—, por no darse entera
al descanso, que vicio considera
si de preciso pasa, cuidadosa
de no incurrir de omisa en el exceso,
a un solo pie librada fía el peso,
y en otro guarda el cálculo pequeño
—despertador reloj del leve sueño—,
porque, si necesario fué admitido,
no pueda dilatarse continuado,
antes interrumpido
del regio sea pastoral cuidado.
¡Oh de la Majestad pensión gravosa,
que aun el menor descuido no perdona!
Causa, quizá, que ha hecho misteriosa,
circular, denotando, la corona,
en círculo dorado,
que el afán es no menos continuado.

El sueño todo, en fin, lo poseía:
todo, en fin, el silencio lo ocupaba:
aun el ladrón dormía;
aun el amante no se desvelaba.

El conticinio casi ya pasando
iba, y la sombra dimidiaba, cuando
de las diurnas tareas fatigados
—y no sólo oprimidos
del afán ponderoso
del corporal trabajo, mas cansados
del deleite también (que también cansa
objeto continuado a los sentidos
aun siendo deleitoso:
que la Naturaleza siempre alterna
ya una, ya otra balanza,
distribuyendo varios ejercicios,
ya al ocio, ya al trabajo destinados,
en el fiel infiel con que gobierna
la aparatosa máquina del mundo)—
así, pues, de profundo
sueño dulce los miembros ocupados,
quedaron los sentidos

The magnanimous bird to Jupiter devoted[7]
—a queen, after all—disdains to give herself
To rest entire, a vice, as she considers,
If at all exceed the requisite;
Concerned lest she incur neglect's excess,
She entrusts her balanced weight to one foot only
And in the other holds a little pebble
—An alarm clock to disturb her so light slumber—
So that, necessity being permitted,
It may not extend itself beyond all measure,
But rather be interrupted
By the burden of her regal pastoral cares.
O heavy weight of Majesty's concern,
Which does not pardon the slightest carelessness!
The mysterious cause perhaps that makes the crown
Circular in shape, to all denoting,
In its golden circle closed,
That royal solicitude is no less endless.

Sleep then at length all things possessed completely;
All things at length then silence dominated:
Even the thief was sleeping;
Even the lover did not lie awake.

The dead of night had almost passed away,
And the shade itself divided, when, fatigued
By the tasks of life quotidian—not only
Oppressed by the weighty care
Of body's work, but tired
By pleasure also (for also can one tire
Of any object subject to the senses,
Even when it gives pleasure:
For Nature always alternates, now one,
Now the other balancing,
In turn distributing diverse pursuits,
To leisure some, to labor others destined,
In the faithful faithlessness with which she governs
The extravagant machinery of the world)—
Thus, then, fully seized
All members by profound and sweetest sleep,
The senses did remain,
If not deprived at least suspended from

---

7. The eagle.

del que ejercicio tienen ordinario
—trabajo, en fin pero trabajo amado,
si hay amable trabajo—,
si privados no, al menos suspendidos,
y cediendo al retrato del contrario
de la vida, que—lentamente armado—
cobarde embiste y vence perezoso
con armas soñolientas,
desde el cayado humilde al cetro altivo,
sin que haya distintivo
que el sayal de la púrpura discierna:
pues su nivel, en todo poderoso,
gradúa por exentas
a ningunas personas,
desde la de a quien tres forman coronas
soberana tïara,
hasta la que pajiza vive choza;
desde la que el Danubio undoso dora,
a la que junco humilde, humilde mora;
y con siempre igual vara
(como, en efecto, imagen poderosa
de la muerte) Morfeo
el sayal mide igual con el brocado.

El alma, pues, suspensa
del exterior gobierno—en que ocupada
en material empleo,
o bien o mal da el día por gastado—
solamente dispensa
remota, si del todo separada
no, a los de muerte temporal opresos
lánguidos miembros, sosegados huesos,
los gajes del calor vegetativo,
el cuerpo siendo, en sosegada calma,
un cadáver con alma,
muerto a la vida y a la muerte vivo,
de lo segundo dando tardas señas
el del reloj humano
vital volante que, si no con mano,
con arterial concierto, unas pequeñas
muestras, pulsando, manifiesta lento
de su bien regulado movimiento.

Esta, pues, miembro rey y centro vivo
de espíritus vitales,

The ordinary activity they have
—Work, to be sure, but work that is belovéd,
If work belovéd can be—
And, yielding to the likeness of the opposite
Of life, which—weaponed stealthily—approaches,
As a coward assaults and conquers as a sluggard,
With soporific arms,
All things from the humble crook to the haughty scepter,
Without making distinction
Between the sackcloth and the purple robe:
For his leveling tool, with power over all,
Will figure no exemptions
For anything that lives,
From her for whom three crowns unite to form
A sovereign tiara
To her who dwells within a hut of straw,
From her who is by the wavy Danube gilded
To her who, humble reed, as humble dwells;
And with always equal measure
(As, in effect, the true and potent image
Of Death), thus Morpheus
Lays equal gauge on sackcloth and brocade.

The soul, thus being suspended
From exterior control—in which employed
In material designs
For good or ill it has the day consumed—
Remote, though not entirely separated,
Unto the languid members,
The tranquil bones, by temporary death
Oppressed, the wage of vegetative heat
Doth grant, the quiet body meanwhile being
A cadaver with a soul,
Dead unto life and unto death alive,
Of the second fact bestowing sluggish signals
The vital flywheel of the human watch,
Which not with manual gesture
But with arterial harmony betrays
Small signs, pulsating, and so manifests
The regulated movement of its being.

This, then, the member royal, the living center
Of the vital spirits all,

127

con su asociado respirante fuelle
—pulmón, que imán del viento es atractivo,
que en movimientos nunca desiguales
o comprimiendo ya, o ya dilatando
el musculoso, claro arcaduz blando,
hace que en él resuelle
el que lo circunscribe fresco ambiente
que impele ya caliente,
y él venga su expulsión haciendo activo
pequeños robos al calor nativo,
algún tiempo llorados,
nunca recuperados,
si ahora no sentidos de su dueño,
que, repetido, no hay robo pequeño—;
éstos, pues, de mayor, como ya digo,
exeptión, uno y otro fiel testigo,
la vida aseguraban,
mientras con mudas voces impugnaban
la información, callados, los sentidos
—con no replicar sólo defendidos—,
y la lengua que, torpe, enmudecía,
con no poder hablar los desmentía. . . .

With its associate, the heaving bellows
—The lung, which is the loadstone to the wind
Attractive, which in ever-equal movements
Now contracting, now expanding, the fine vessel
Both muscular and pliant, brings about
That in it may respire
The circumambient freshness that surrounds it
And quickens it with warmth;
And in its breathing action it commits
Petty thefts upon its native heat,
One day to be lamented,
Never to be recovered,
If not yet apperceived by the possessor:
Indeed, repeated, no theft can be petty—
These, thus, as I've said, proved great exceptions,
Each one as faithful witness testifying
Assured continuing life,
While the senses with mute voices contradicted
In their silence the very information given
—Prevented only in their not replying—
And the tongue which—heavy, forced into silence—
Being of speech deprived, gave them the lie. . . .

Bibliography

EDITIONS

Labé, Louise. *Oeuvres*. Edited by Charles Boy. Geneva: Slatkine Reprints, 1968; reprint of the edition of Paris: A. Lemerre, 1887, 2 vols.

Stampa, Gaspara, and Veronica Franco. *Rime*. Edited by Abdelkader Salza. Bari: Laterza, 1913.

Sor Juana Inés de la Cruz. *Obras completas*. Edited by Alfonso Méndez Plancarte and Alberto G. Salceda. 4 vols. Mexico City: Fondo de Cultura Económica, 1951–57.

CRITICAL WORKS CONCERNING THE POETS

Bassanese, Fiora A. *Gaspara Stampa*. Boston: G. K. Hall, 1982.

Clamurro, William. "Sor Juana Inés de la Cruz Reads her Portrait." *Revista de Estudios Hispánicos* 20 (No. 1 1986).

Donadoni, Eugenio. *Gaspara Stampa, Vita e opera*. Messina: Principato, 1919.

Guernelli, Giovanni. *Gaspara Stampa, Louise Labé y Sor Juana Inés de la Cruz: Triptico renacentista barroco*. San Juan: Universidad de Puerto Rico Press, 1972.

Graves, Robert. "Juana de Asbaje." In *The Crowning Privilege*. London: Cassell, 1955.

Harvey, Lawrence E. *The Aesthetics of the Renaissance Love Sonnet: An Essay on the Art of the Sonnet in the Poetry of Louise Labé*. Geneva: Droz, 1962.

O'Connor, Dorothy. *Louis Labé: Sa vie et son oeuvre*. Geneva: Slatkine Reprints, 1972; reprint of the edition of Paris: Presses Françaises, 1926.

Pfandl, Ludwig. *Sor Juana Inés de la Cruz: La Décima Musa de México*.

Trans. from the German by J. A. Ortega y Medina. Mexico City: UNAM, 1963.

Toffanin, Giuseppe. "Gaspara Stampa." In *Storia letteraria: Il Cinquecento.* Milan: Vallardi, 1929.

Vitiello, Justin. "Gaspara Stampa: The Ambiguities of Martyrdom." *Modern Language Notes* 90 (January 1975): 58–71.

OTHER WORKS CITED

Graves, Robert. *The White Goddess,* enl. edition. New York: Vintage, 1972.

Grierson, H. J. C., ed. *The Poems of John Donne.* 2 vols. Oxford: Oxford University Press, 1912.

Hatzfeld, Helmut. *Estudios sobre el barroco.* Madrid: Gredos, 1964.

Hauser, Arnold. *Mannerism: The Crisis of the Renaissance and the Origin of Modern Art.* 2 vols. London: Routledge and Kegan Paul, 1965.

Mourgues, Odette de. *Metaphysical, Baroque, and Précieux Poetry.* Oxford: Oxford University Press, 1953.

Rougemont, Denis de. *Love in the Western World.* Rev. ed. Garden City, N.Y.: Doubleday, 1957.

Skrine, Peter. *The Baroque.* New York: Holmes and Meier, 1978.

Sypher, Wylie. *Four Stages of Renaissance Style.* Garden City, N.Y.: Doubleday, 1955.

Warnke, F. J. *Versions of Baroque.* New Haven: Yale University Press, 1972.

Wellek, René *Concepts of Criticism.* New Haven: Yale University Press, 1963.

Woolf, Virginia. *A Room of One's Own.* New York: Harcourt, Brace, 1929.

Index of
Foreign Language Titles

Index of English Titles